STRATEGIC PROJECT MANAGEMENT

STRATEGIC SUCCESS SERIES

STRATEGIC PROJECT MANAGEMENT

PAUL ROBERTS

First published in Great Britain and the United States in 2012 by Kogan Page Limited

120 Pentonville Road	1518 Walnut Street, Suite 1100	4737/23 Ansari Road
London N1 9JN	Philadelphia PA 19102	Daryaganj
United Kingdom	USA	New Delhi 110002
www.koganpage.com		India

© Paul Roberts, 2012

The right of Paul Roberts to be identified as the author of this work has been asserted by him in accordance with the Copyright, Designs and Patents Act 1988.

ISBN   978 0 7494 6433 2
E-ISBN   978 0 7494 6434 9

British Library Cataloguing-in-Publication Data

A CIP record for this book is available from the British Library.

Library of Congress Cataloging-in-Publication Data
Roberts, Paul, 1964–
    Strategic project management : creating the conditions for success / Paul Roberts.
      p. cm.
    ISBN 978-0-7494-6433-2 – ISBN 978-0-7494-6434-9   1. Project management.
2. Strategic planning.   I. Title.
    HD69.P75R634 2012
    658.4'04–dc23
                                                            2011051472

Typeset by Graphicraft Limited, Hong Kong
Printed and bound in India by Replika Press Pvt Ltd

**To my children, Matthew and Ruby,
who fill our lives with energy, humour and love.**

CONTENTS

BIOGRAPHY

Paul Roberts has been managing projects for over 20 years and is a founding director of Fifthday Longview Limited (**www.fifthday.com**), one of the world's leading – and most innovative – project management consultancies, providing expertise, education and resource. He has worked with some of the world's largest, most influential companies, and many of the smallest, both public and private, helping them all to embed the principles, techniques and culture of effective project management. This is his third book.

ACKNOWLEDGEMENTS

I am continually grateful for the friendship, guidance and opportunity provided by the customers with whom I have formed such a close partnership over the years. As always, I would like to thank the many associates of Fifthday Longview Limited who help us inject real-world experience into our company. And special thanks to Nicola de Jong, Matthew Smith and their wonderful colleagues at Kogan Page.

PREFACE

My interest in writing began as a youngster with a play called *Steve Zeltar Investigates*. The plot, such as it was, focused on the solving of a murder, the subject of which was conveniently laid out on the carpet before the hero. The body, he discovered, had been subjected to 13 separate and different mortal wounds, including, but not limited to, stabbing, gunshots, strangulation and poisoning. By happy coincidence, there were also 13 suspects, each of whom had a motive. So as it turned out, Steve Zeltar didn't have much to investigate. Everyone was the murderer.

I would have forgotten Steve had it not been for the premise for this book. I was keen to understand why projects really fail, and, in recalling the times I had been asked to investigate, could think of none where there was a single cause. In every case there were multiple reasons, each with a connection to someone in the organization who had, or had not, done something important. Again, everyone was the murderer.

But why would anyone *want* a project to fail? I hypothesized that projects fail for the very same single reason that they exist: we *allow* them to. I considered some research listing the common causes of project failure.[1] These included:

- bad communication between relevant parties;
- lack of planning of schedules, resources and activities;
- no quality control;
- milestones being missed;
- inadequate coordination of resources;
- costs spiralling out of control;
- mismanagement of progress;
- overall poor management;
- supplier skills overstretched;
- supplier under-resourced;
- insufficient measurable outputs;
- inconsistent supplier resource.

It occurred to me that each item on the list was the *symptom* of a failed project, not its cause. I wanted to know what had *allowed* the project to get to the point where milestones were being missed, where resources were being inadequately coordinated, and where there was bad communication between relevant parties. I suspected that what lay beneath were behavioural failures of the institutions in which the projects were being incubated and conducted.

I considered some of the project failures I myself had witnessed or investigated, and began to realize that they were destined to fail *simply because of their environment*. I decided I must better understand the cultural characteristics which constituted a 'poor' institutional environment, so that my colleagues and I might better recognize and describe them to others.

I formed this characterization around 10 'myths', each of which I had heard someone say, each of which had pre-dated or pre-empted the failure of a project. I tested it: the audit trail of the failure of every project led back to corporate and individual behaviours born of a belief in one or more of these myths:

Myth 1: If we can manage a business, we can manage a project.
Myth 2: We can do everything we set our minds to.
Myth 3: A great project manager will bring success.
Myth 4: Everyone knows what we want to achieve.
Myth 5: Great ideas need no justification.
Myth 6: Nothing can be allowed to change.
Myth 7: Activity equals productivity.
Myth 8: Our suppliers share our objectives.
Myth 9: By reporting progress, we're controlling it.
Myth 10: We'll deal best with problems as they arise.

This book is structured around understanding each of these myths, and helping to mitigate the risk of allowing a continued belief in them to affect your own behaviour and that of your colleagues, leaders and managers. Having understood how each may be overcome, the final chapter suggests an approach for introducing improvements across an organization. In this way, project management becomes a strategic tool, not just a means of tackling tactical issues and opportunities as they arise.

There are several online resources to support the book. Amongst others, these include a series of templates to facilitate the justification and control of individual projects, tools to assist in the planning and tracking of a portfolio of projects, some materials to help assess the maturity of the organization's project management, and a ready-made list of benefits to assist in the cost-justification of any project management improvements your organization is seeking to implement.

I believe that, in using this book and the online resources, individuals will become better able to employ projects as the vehicles which deliver their organization's strategy. By creating the conditions which lead to successful change, institutions will be transformed into those which move forward because of – not in spite of – the huge investments they routinely make in projects.

Additional resources to accompany the book are available on Kogan Page's *Strategic Success* website:
www.koganpage.com/strategicsuccess

Note

[1] *Spikes Cavell research in finance sector, sponsored by BULL, 1998*

INTRODUCTION

What is a 'failed' project?

A European country's Department for Transport invested heavily in the design and delivery of a toll road to ease congestion on a major motorway. Much of the considerable investment was to be offset by the levy from the toll.

This was a civil engineering project of exceptional proportion involving multiple contractors, huge budgets and new technologies. The combination of such risks required the appointment of a project manager with proven experience, competence and resolve.

As the project progressed, the selected individual and their team faced and overcame extraordinary logistical, operational and geographic challenges. They met their obligations to deliver the project for their client on time and on budget. The road itself was considered to be of the most advanced quality in the world, employing materials and technologies which could reduce accidents, muffle traffic noise and maximize the effective evacuation of rainwater. The project won an award for on-site safety.

To much acclaim, the road was declared open. The project manager and their team enjoyed the plaudits they received. At that time, the project was considered to have been a success.

Years later, the number of vehicles using the toll road was still considerably lower than had been expected. In order to achieve payback within the desired period the toll levy had to be set at a relatively high level. Given that the cost of fuel had increased substantially during the intervening years, many drivers (especially those delivering freight) decided that they would rather tolerate the risk of a delay than pay to avoid it.

The way in which we describe success and failure is of fundamental importance and depends explicitly on whom you ask. The Minister for Transport would never have admitted that the project had failed, yet it had certainly not succeeded in accruing the receipts expected by the Treasury. Nor had it achieved the significant reduction in congestion for which motorists had hoped. Yet at the point at which they left the project, the project manager would have considered it successful.

We might equally observe projects which failed according to many traditional measures, yet which turned out to be huge successes. The epic film, *Titanic*, produced and directed by James Cameron, ran significantly over budget and was thought likely to make a loss of at least $100 million. Not only that, but its premiere was delayed by almost six months and many observers had written it off. Yet, despite such delays and budget excesses, it went on to become (at that time) the highest grossing film of all time, achieving global revenues of $1.8 billion. And if that were not sufficient measure of success, it garnered 11 of its 14 Academy Award nominations. Now no one is at all concerned that it was delayed, delivered late and supremely over budget. What we recall is that the venture was justified by the end it achieved. We do projects to bring about benefits of some sort. Sometimes, those benefits are worth waiting longer for, or are deserving of greater investment than originally planned.

So as we consider the *real* causes of project failure, it is crucial that we understand 'failure' to mean that insufficient benefits were realized to justify the investment. We should place less emphasis on the traditional 'time', 'cost' and 'quality' measures and instead ask ourselves, 'Was it all *worth* it?'

When do we know a project has failed?

A project is a management vehicle to deliver something – a computer system, a bridge, a building, a new set of working practices – which leads to the realization of benefits. If we use the definition of failure above, it is often only possible to know that a project has ultimately failed when the project environment is no longer present to do anything about it. We may have to wait many months, or years, to know whether the investment was ultimately justified; and by that time, who still cares? Realistically, interest will have waned in favour of the next big project into which energies and investments are directed.

In my experience, few organizations seek to know whether the realized benefits ultimately outweigh the accumulated investment. Those organizations that *do* carry out a project review traditionally do so immediately after the project has delivered – which is way too early to measure true success or failure. At best, all they succeed in judging is the management of the project, not its outcome. This view is supported by an analysis of the research that has been conducted to understand why projects fail. Because the data is often gathered at the point of project closure, and not when the benefits have been measured, it commonly points to failures in project *management*, but not necessarily the failure of the project itself. It would be possible for a project to have been judged a failure at the time of closure, yet years later to have been deemed a success. I worked with an organization who decided to fix a data processing problem with a highly automated solution. Partway through the project, it was realized that the automation was proving too complex to deliver. A compromise was agreed by which a temporary member of staff was hired once a month to manually transfer a list of data from one computer to another. Given that money had been wasted on a solution which was abandoned, the project was considered to have failed. However, the 'workaround' soon became permanent; although inelegant, it was widely recognized to be a simple and cost-effective way of fixing the original problem.

A further disadvantage of judging success or failure at the point of delivery is that we obtain a skewed perspective: instead of understanding why projects *generally* fail, we assess why one *specific* project *might* have failed. We form the dubious assumption that the characteristics of one project can tell us something reliable about the state of all projects in the wider organization.

But many projects never even get to their respective point of delivery. A study conducted in the European Union identified that almost a quarter were cancelled before they delivered, the vast majority partway during their development. By my own definition of failure above, they failed: insufficient benefits were realized to justify the investment. Yet in the case of a cancelled project, there are *some* crumbs of comfort to be enjoyed. Judged at the time of cancellation, the management of the project may be deemed to have been successful by curtailing the continued investment in what was foreseen to be a loss-making venture. The project failed, but the consequences on the sponsoring organization were not as catastrophic as they might have been. So some projects fail better than others.

Who is at fault for failure?

When a project succeeds, it delivers value to the organization which sponsored it. When it fails, it can have an equal and opposite effect, having the potential to destroy staff morale, customer confidence and shareholder value. We *expect* a project to affect the organization. However, it is equally true that the organization will affect the project. Projects are connected to the organizations within which they are conducted – they inherit its people, its processes, its resources and its *culture*. If that culture is insufficiently capable of understanding and delivering projects, it is possible to see that many project failures have their root cause in the institutions that sponsor them. The projects themselves cannot be held solely accountable for their own failure.

Once a project is underway, much of the governance it needs is contained within it. So the plan, the people, the controls are all brought under its umbrella. This is, of course, one of the great advantages of having a particular way of managing projects: the amount of governance needed is geared to the riskiness of the project itself. However, much of what will most affect a project are those strategic decisions taken outside its boundaries. Whether it should start, how much of the organization's money it will be allowed to consume, who will be held accountable for its effective management... these are beyond the authority of the project itself to determine, and should be driven by strategic considerations. So, although the individuals within a project may take decisions which lead to its eventual failure, the institution that gave them their authority must be held accountable. Yes, projects sometimes fail their institutions, but institutions fail their projects too.

How do institutions fail their projects?

The contribution institutions make to the failure of their projects is often almost entirely innocent, but not excusable. Whilst most now recognize project management as a necessary and structured discipline, some continue to believe that the guarantee of success lies within the control of the projects themselves. These institutions know, or have in place, little of the strategic governance surrounding their projects that is needed to help germinate, incubate and produce lasting value.

I believe that the argument for effective management *inside* a project has been largely won. Sure, there remain many organizations who continue to deny the need, but they are in the minority. The biggest hurdle to overcome now is to persuade a much broader management audience that their organizations have *two* purposes: to operate effectively, and to change effectively. They are familiar with the former; but of the latter, I believe many still have much to learn. They consider the need to change to be intermittent rather than a permanent pressure. As a consequence, they are uncomfortable with and unused to the need for a robust, embedded and permanent culture to deliver continuous strategic change. This is why I suggest that they *innocently* fail their projects: they simply possess too little of the machinery or language of change to know any better. This becomes inexcusable when projects continue to fail and the endemic causes remain unknown or unresolved.

In the chapters that follow, we'll explore 10 hugely significant ways in which institutions can increase the likelihood of success for their projects, and in so doing, achieve their strategic objectives. I've chosen to describe them by means of 'imperatives' which, if understood and embedded in the culture, will help to develop the behaviour and practice of the organization. Here's how each topic will be covered:

- *The imperative and the myth*: what is meant by the imperative, and how might the institution be presently deceiving itself?
- *Case study*: to illuminate the matter being considered in the chapter.
- *What this means*: what are the specific issues raised by the Case study?
- *The consequences of ignoring the imperative*: what is the likely impact on the wider organization?
- *The solutions*: what are the practical ways by which to address the identified problems?
- *Conclusion*: what will be the positive – and negative – consequences of investing in the solutions?

It is my sincere wish that you do not recognize in yourself or your organization too many of the characteristics I am about to describe. But should it be the case, draw some comfort from knowing that you are taking a crucial first step towards using individual projects not only to deliver specific benefits, but to contribute to the achievement of strategic change.

SUMMARY

- A project is a management vehicle to deliver something which leads to the realization of benefits.
- Sometimes, those benefits are worth waiting longer for, or are deserving of greater investment than originally planned.
- What constitutes success or failure depends on whom and when you ask.
- Judging success or failure immediately after the point of delivery will succeed only in assessing the management of the project and the quality of the deliverable, not whether the benefits were worth the investment.
- Project 'failure' means that insufficient benefits were eventually realized to justify the investment.
- A cancelled project is still a failed project, but the impact is reduced by timely intervention.
- Since every project that fails does so for a unique combination of reasons, it is wrong to assume that the characteristics of one failed project can tell us something reliable about the state of all projects in the wider organization.
- Projects are connected to the organizations within which they are conducted – many project failures have their root cause in the institutions that sponsor them.
- The most important decisions about a project are taken outside its boundaries.
- The pressure to compete and adapt is a permanent one: in the same way that institutions need a robust, embedded and permanent governance to operate, so too do they need one to achieve strategic *change*.

CHAPTER ONE

DON'T MISTAKE THE 'BUSINESS AS USUAL' MINDSET FOR THAT SUITED TO DELIVERING CHANGE

This chapter covers:

- the problems which will arise from failing to treat projects as shared, organization-wide endeavours;
- the consequences for the whole institution when such failures become endemic;
- the ways in which organizations may approach projects differently from that of 'business as usual'.

Many organizations are extremely good at what they do. Yours may be one of them. Yet a good number of such organizations have been severely compromised by a flawed assumption. They believe:

Myth 1: If we can manage a business, we can manage a project.

In this chapter, we will seek to debunk this myth and show how a different mindset is needed to deliver sustainable, beneficial change.

CASE STUDY

For well over a century, a well-respected global organization had been operating very successfully in a highly competitive market. I met with them when they were conducting a large, transformational project to develop a commercially robust internet portal through which their customers could access their products and services. The project had been underway for some months but was seriously out of control. I was asked to conduct a health check to uncover the problems and help the organization overcome them.

A lunch had been arranged for the 17 people who were to participate. As the table was being cleared away in preparation for the afternoon's review session, I asked which one of those present was the project manager. Five people put up their hands. It took only a matter of seconds for everyone in the room to recognize the problem, yet after 20 minutes' noisy debate, they were still no closer to knowing who was in charge.

It was no coincidence that the project required the participation of five separate departments. Each had assumed responsibility for their particular part of the project, precipitating the creation of five disconnected, departmentally ring-fenced sets of activity. All of this was in place of what should have been one shared endeavour from which they would all benefit.

Whilst one might conclude that the project was failing for lack of the coordinating presence of a single project manager, it was merely one symptom of an underlying cause. *The business made the flawed assumption described in my opening paragraph.* It thought that it could deliver an organization-wide change using a structure which had been designed and populated with people recruited to do something entirely different. Of course, it would be reasonably straightforward to put in place a single project manager to plan, monitor and control the work of them all. But until the organization addressed the underlying behaviours that had *allowed* such an important initiative to progress without some simple, coordinated management, every successive project would trip up in exactly the same way.

What this means

Like the Case study above, there is a great likelihood that your organization has been designed, built and populated to do one thing well: to deliver its products or services, whatever they may be, to whomsoever you serve. So you may work within a hospital which delivers healthcare to patients. You may work for a bank which delivers savings and lending products to retail customers. You may work for a branch of government that delivers policy. In each case, your organization has been constructed around the competencies to do these things every day for as long as the institution continues to exist. This is what we call 'business as usual', commonly shortened to BAU.

We design and build a tailored organization structure to manage BAU. The people who populate it are partitioned into departments according to their skills and knowledge. Departments may include sales, marketing, IT, finance, operations and any number of others relating to the specialist nature of the organization in question. Whilst sharing an interest in the wider organization's general objectives, each department is motivated and incentivized very differently, each according to the specific role they play within the whole. Coordinated from the top, there is an expectation that the combination of departments working in harmony will facilitate the daily operation of the organization. But we are quite wrong to presuppose that it will also be suitable for delivering *changes*. Why is that?

The organization's structure

If we make demands of an organizational structure for which it was not designed, it should not surprise us if it fails to meet our expectations. In the Case study, the business's organization structure was partitioned into departments to serve its BAU purpose, just as one might expect. But faced with a project requiring an unusual liaison between a unique combination of departments, the participants fell into the only configuration they knew. They had no knowledge or experience of an alternative model which would suit the project, so they each took on the activities in which they believed themselves to be qualified.

An equally unpalatable alternative to dividing up the project across each department is when an organization places it all within the boundaries of only one of them. A common, dangerous and exasperating example of this is when projects are 'done by the IT department'. It is incredibly rare for there to be any project whose stakeholders all work within the IT department. The participants needed in even the most technical of projects will include those who are funding it, or will use the project's end deliverable. Even the upgrade of a piece of basic software requires the training of those outside IT who will need to use it.

It is seriously dangerous to assume that there is any such thing as an 'IT project'. To believe that there is places an unnecessary and false constraint on the scope of the project, and provides other essential stakeholders with a great excuse to back away. The consequence? IT is blamed for the failure of a project that required – but lacked – the participation of others.

However, it would be remiss not to point out that for some organizations, projects *are* their BAU. For instance, a company with whom I worked delivered complex software solutions to the banking industry. Every time a sale was agreed, a project with the client was initiated to develop, test and implement their new product. The organization had long ago identified that project management was a competence on which it depended. For this reason, the culture was very much geared towards the management of projects, and the line structure reflected it. So there was a 'project management department' populated with project specialists. Departmental meetings were few since cross-functional project meetings were more suited to the nature of the work and people were incentivized to meet project objectives as well as departmental targets.

Project ownership and direction

In the Case study, although the discussion about who was the project manager helped to bring some issues to the surface, a more substantial question remained: who was the *sponsor*? That five departments had been able to divide the project into an unmanageable tangle of activity was a problem which the introduction of a project manager would have actually done little to resolve. The board, in treating the project as though it was BAU, had failed to assign it to a single, competent owner on whose shoulders they could place the responsibility for delivery of the benefits. Had a single sponsor been appointed to own, direct and deliver the change on behalf of the business, the means would have been in place to design a tailored organization structure, including a project manager, to clarify and articulate the vision, and lead the business to a successful conclusion.

Planning and control

The absence of a sponsor and project manager resulted in a failure by everyone to comprehend the project as a single, shared endeavour. The need for the project had arisen from a planning session conducted at board level. On agreement, the board treated the instruction to commission the project in exactly the same way as any BAU activity: they passed the instruction down the line to 'make it happen'. The message was received by at least the five departments who eventually became involved, and each went about progressing it in the only way they knew how – by planning the activities that their department would need to undertake. Where one project had been anticipated, five were being developed. Figure 1.1 illustrates the situation.

FIGURE 1.1

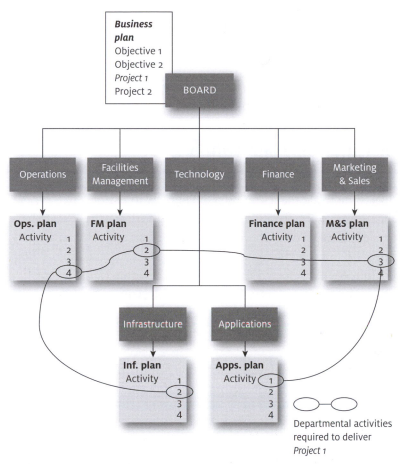

Departmental activities
required to deliver
Project 1

The arrangement had a consequent effect. Not only were instructions being delegated *down* the line, problems and questions were being escalated *up* it. Departmental meetings at which the business traditionally addressed problems and questions were already in place and had been for decades (some of them for over a century!). There was a bi-weekly sales meeting, a weekly IT operations forum, a monthly finance meeting and countless others. Yet there was no management vehicle to expose and resolve problems facing their cross-functional project. At my suggestion that there should be, there was almost universal horror at the prospect of 'another meeting'. Yet was it reasonable that a large, risky and costly investment in a project should be exposed to any less control than a department?

A further consequence of passing projects down the line in this way was to allow the departments themselves to determine their relative priority. This in turn led to a huge disparity across the business; some departments placed great emphasis on the success of a specific project, whilst others did the exact opposite.

Incentives and motivation

In any well-run organization, we don't simply tell people what to do; we motivate them and offer incentives to perform well. Those incentives and motivations are designed for each specific department in the BAU organization. For instance, sales people are usually rewarded on the volume and value of sales that they make. This encourages them to sell more and clearly works in the interest of the organization's growth. But does that same incentive work in the interests of a project? Why should a sales person want to participate in a project if it takes them away from doing what they are employed and motivated to do? The incentives to successfully use projects to deliver changes to the organization are quite different from those employed to maintain and grow it.

Individual competencies

The Case study serves to illustrate how an organization's physical line structure is principally designed around delivering BAU. Each department or division within it is populated with people who have the skills, knowledge and experience to do some very specific jobs. Unless there are change management professionals contained somewhere within the organization (and occasionally there are), where will the competence to run or sponsor a project be found? Are the skills, knowledge and experience needed to deliver change absent in those who deliver BAU?

In some cases, the skills needed to manage BAU are similar to those needed to deliver a successful project. For instance, managers who run departments are expected to have the skills to plan time, to cost-justify expenditure, to build a team and to manage risk. But the deep-rooted personal qualities, the knowledge of project-specific techniques and the experience of having applied them are not automatically present in every manager. More importantly, nor is the unique combination of change management competencies commonly found in a *single* individual. So whilst it is true to say that many people have the *potential* to manage or sponsor projects competently, not all begin with the full complement of skills, knowledge, experience, qualities or confidence to do so. So delegating the management of a project to someone who happens to be a good *general* manager may do little to lessen the persistent risk of failure.

The consequences of ignoring the imperative

The Case study suggested some of the effects of managing change as though it were any other business activity. Within the project itself, which is where efforts were made to address the problems, delay, confusion and waste were obvious consequences. However, when multiplied by the considerable number of projects the organization had underway at the same time (and which were suffering in the same way) the impact was magnified such that it was felt by the business. Several tremors combined to create real instability. Some of the institutional consequences of managing projects in the same way as the daily operation of the business are as follows:

- Business as usual can become compromised – as more interest is devoted to failing or inefficiently run projects, attention is drawn away from the very business we are seeking to maintain and develop (and which is funding those projects). Conversely, the following may be true...
- You'll do projects in your spare time – unless projects are discretely and efficiently scoped, planned and resourced, the attention of the workforce will remain focused on BAU. Projects will become funded from 'goodwill' rather than the ring-fenced budget they deserve.

- Your reputation with customers will suffer – this is especially the case if the products and services you offer are delivered to your customers by means of projects. When customers depend on a delivery from you on time, on budget and to their specification, any failure of that project to meet their standards is not something that can be kept within the confines of the business.
- Your costs will escalate – projects are undertaken because they are necessary or essential for the continuation or growth of the business. Their abandonment is not seen as an option. The consequence of failing to adequately manage them is that those projects consume increasing resources. If the time arrives when the endeavour does have to be abandoned, the financial and other costs can of course be enormous. For the business, there may well be a direct hit on profitability with implications on shareholder value and investor relations.
- Others will use their change management capabilities as a competitive advantage over you – their innovations will be delivered more quickly or economically, and they will delight the market with their ability to deliver their products and services more efficiently than you.
- The change competence in your organization will not grow – those who do have some competence will either burn out from the pressures of working in an environment which is not suited to the effective delivery of change, or they will seek positions in organizations where change agents have an opportunity to work in a culture which is supportive and conducive to success.

Simply summarized, if change management remains unrecognized as a specialist discipline in its own right, there is a high likelihood that the organization will fail to deliver the changes it needs to stay, or become, competitive.

The solutions

In any organization, different jobs require different tools. The challenge of managing change requires a unique and specialized toolkit

FIGURE 1.2

which may not presently exist in the organization. Unfortunately, for many organizations, instead of investing in the tools most suited to the challenges, they seek to get by with what they already have. And if all you have is a hammer, everything looks like a nail.

The institutional toolkit to manage change is illustrated in the diagram in Figure 1.2.

Prioritize and manage your portfolio of projects

As we will discover in the next chapter, the amount of change your organization wants or needs will nearly always outstrip the resources available to deliver it. At some point, any institution that is undergoing some form of change – and that includes nearly every one of them – will have to decide which projects are of greatest importance.

A 'Change Management Team' (CMT) can help the organization to make such decisions. It will serve as the senior-most authority for change in the business, overseeing the portfolio of projects, delegating them to individual sponsors, and coordinating them such that the business delivers its change agenda. In other words, it is a body which does for change what other operational bodies do for BAU. We'll return to consider the CMT in the next chapter.

It may take some time, and a change of perspective, to see what may be a large part of your business as a list of prioritized projects. Thereafter, it is crucial to steer that portfolio of projects continuously towards what you consider a successful outcome. Businesses invest in the ordered, incremental growth of BAU; so too should they construct a portfolio of projects which is affordable, focused and achievable.

When the list has been identified, do not assume that its promotion across the organization will result in its delivery. As the Case study illustrates, left to its own devices a BAU structure will deal with a project in the only way it knows how: by tearing it apart into departmental chunks of work.

Instead, assign each project to a single, safe pair of hands...

Appoint authoritative project sponsors/owners

There is a difference between managing a project and directing it. Direction has more to do with clarifying and articulating the goal rather than planning a means of achieving it. It is about ownership of the project's objective for change, and setting the direction in which the project will need to head if the benefits are to be achieved. By contrast, the managers of the projects will take instruction from those who direct them, developing plans and motivating resources to develop the projects' deliverables.

So, before considering who may be best placed to *manage* the project, think first about who in the organization needs to *direct* it. A single sponsor must be identified on whom accountability for the successful delivery of the change may be placed. Without this single individual, at best everyone seeks to instruct the project manager, leaving them faced with a confusing and often incompatible set of targets. At worst, no one is held liable for a successful outcome and the project manager takes the project wherever they wish or can. It is as if the ship has a captain, but no one to tell them where to sail.

As future chapters will explain, it is likely that these project sponsors will be rare beasts. Not only must they have the authority to secure the necessary funding and engagement, but they must also possess leadership and change management skills which qualify them to head up a project in addition to departments. This is not to say that the heads of departments would not qualify for the role – far from it – but they will need to engage a different set of competencies to direct a project. Put another way, they will be your organization's superheroes, one minute using their specific subject-matter expertise to run a business function, the next delivering a significant, organization-wide change.

Not every senior manager will immediately have the competence or mindset to discharge such a role. But an organization's capacity for delivering change is as much limited by its number of sponsors as it is by its cash. So as the organization decides which change initiatives it wishes to pursue, it must also identify a list of competent sponsors to whom the authority for each selected project will be delegated. It is a serious question to be asking of your own business: who are your organization's qualified sponsors?

Once known, these individuals – not departments – may be granted the authority to cost-justify, recruit and manage the resources the projects require to deliver the change.

Robustly initiate and cost-justify every project

It is not at all unusual for projects to materialize in the business as though they were beamed down from the Starship Enterprise. They arrive almost without invitation. The question as to where projects come from will consume a future chapter, and more. Whatever their source, whether because it is someone's pet obsession, a regulatory change with no option for avoidance, a commercial opportunity or a cost-reduction initiative, every project must be justified. There are several reasons for this:

- Each individual project represents a balance of investment versus return. We may feel positive about the potential investment, but if we are to know that it is a viable proposal, only a clearly articulated argument should persuade the organization to part with its money.
- The fortunes of the project will change. Even though there may be a clear-cut case in favour of pursuing a mandatory project over which we have little choice, the investment we make in it is still within our control. A project's business case helps the sponsor to manage both the benefits *and* the costs.
- The business has a choice as to which projects it chooses to pursue. As we will see in the next chapter, even if it has the will to take on every opportunity, it is unlikely to have the resource. The cost-justification helps the organization select and prioritize its projects.
- The development of a formal, structured project cost-justification creates with it the opportunity for its approval. This effectively ensures that projects are subjected to at least one considered decision-making point beyond which the enterprise is prevented from moving until or unless it is approved.

Orientate the organization to accommodate projects

It takes an organization to successfully deliver a project, but the organization must be designed to do so. As the Case study suggested, unless the business is 'change literate', the BAU structure and mindset will be inappropriate.

The physical structure and the roles and responsibilities of the participants in a change-literate organization are different. A project is a management environment with the internal authority to make the right decisions at the right time; however, it also affects the company itself. Consequently, the company should examine how it provides resources to projects at the same time as conducting essential BAU activity.

A common complaint is that a combination of projects and BAU pulls too many people in too many directions. Priorities are unclear;

all the stops are pulled out for an important project until something happens to compromise the operation of the rest of the business. At that point the project (much to the chagrin of its sponsor) is pushed to one side. Organizations with a strong emphasis on day-to-day, operational excellence often consider projects to be of secondary importance. This has some merit as it is BAU which funds projects. However, when this attitude becomes endemic, projects lose their sponsorship in favour of operational firefighting. This is not healthy in a progressive organization seeking to adapt and grow.

A resource pool is a group of people within a single management structure, usually with common skills. We have already referred to them as departments or functions. Effective resource pool management helps to balance the competing demands on those people to conduct effective BAU whilst at the same time releasing enough of them to deliver a portfolio of value-focused projects.

The sponsor responsible for staffing a new project requests resources from a wide variety of internal and, possibly, external sources. In this way, they obtain the unique mix of skills, knowledge, experience and character they believe will serve the project well. This creates a further responsibility for the heads of departments from whom the resources have been picked. They have not only to meet their BAU commitments, but must also maintain a stock of people with enough competence and capacity to contribute to projects.

Resource pool management is needed to ensure that both BAU and projects have enough people of the quality they need at the right time. There are at least two organizational models which can facilitate this: the free market and the regulated market.

The free market

Having been given authority to deliver a successful outcome, the sponsors attempt to secure the resources they need from a variety of sources, both internal and external. External sources such as third-party resource suppliers may well require a bigger investment, but the sponsors have accountability for delivering a commercially viable outcome. As long as the project's benefits outweigh its costs, they can argue in favour of employing external resources.

FIGURE 1.3

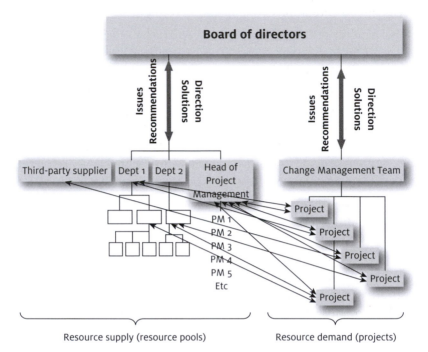

Resource supply (resource pools)   Resource demand (projects)

Internal suppliers such as those in Department 1 and Department 2 in Figure 1.3 can work in much the same way as an external provider, with one significant exception. Although they are resource pools, many of these internal departments must also deliver successful BAU, so most department managers are charged with managing the supply of resources to projects *and* BAU activity.

Matters can become more complicated when a department is subjected to requests from more than one project. Such competition can be regulated.

The regulated market

This structure differs in two important ways from the free market model:

● The multiple supply and demand relationships between project and resource pool managers have been rationalized through a single 'resource management function'.

FIGURE 1.4

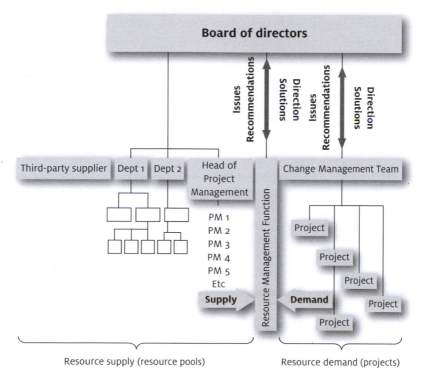

- The source of escalation for issues arising from shortages (or oversupply) of resources no longer rests with the resource pool managers but with the resource management function.

Having a resource management function does not remove the need for the resource pool managers to nurture their teams. Nor does it mean that they should not plan for future project and BAU demands. It can, however, add some considerable benefits:

- forward planning of resource numbers so that cross-department recruitment campaigns can be managed;
- increased negotiating power with third-party resource providers;
- improved arbitration where resource conflicts arise;
- skills management (using skills profiles for selection rather than availability alone);
- decreases in the incidence of potentially available resources being reserved for the personal use of their department (resource pool) managers.

To make this happen, the resource management function must:

- plan and maintain forecasts for company-wide resource demands based on regularly gathered project resource plans;
- plan and maintain forecasts for company-wide resource supply based on regularly gathered department resource plans;
- match resource demand from potential and existing projects with the potential and existing supply available from internal and external resource pools;
- identify, report and respond to resource supply and demand trends;
- plan, coordinate and support recruitment campaigns across the organization.

At the end of a year, it should be possible to judge the function's success by measuring:

- to what extent resource utilization has been maximized;
- the availability of a current, company-wide resource plan;
- whether, at any time, all projects have a forecast of resource demand and all departments have a forecast of resource supply.

Both models recognize that projects are usually neither owned by, nor contained within, a single department. They are shared endeavours that draw on the skills, knowledge and experience of a variety of stakeholders who each have differing expectations of success. As the Case study suggests, projects cut across the departmental divides. Creating a matrix and managing resources through both line and project structures is called matrix management. When used effectively, it allows organizations to deliver better BAU and projects simultaneously. Without it, projects are often the first casualty as BAU takes priority.

There are several consequences of either model. First, if resources are to be engaged in projects for only a relatively short time, it may be necessary for resource pool managers to 'backfill' their positions so as not to compromise the continued running of the department. Second, it may be necessary to conduct performance appraisals with input specifically sourced from the projects in which people have worked in addition to their BAU activity.

In both models there is also a 'head of project management' who can play a key role in a matrix management environment.

The head of project management is principally a resource pool manager responsible for managing the project management personnel needed to satisfy the demands of sponsors as they seek project managers for emerging projects. Like any other resource pool manager, this person will manage the longer-term needs of the department by recruiting, developing and retaining the best project managers required to maintain a healthy pool of personnel.

The head of project management should be an experienced person who can contribute to the continued development and application of the company's approach to project management. Even so, if the resource pool is small, this may not be a full-time role and could be performed by a project manager in addition to existing duties.

The head of project management should not become involved in BAU or project matters other than those for which they already have specific responsibilities. Challenges arising within individual projects should be managed by those projects. The head of project management is, however, expected to prevent or manage any matters related to the efficacy, supply or quality of project management personnel.

The head of project management's specific responsibilities are to:

- supply project managers to project sponsors when given a demand forecast;
- manage the pool of resources effectively within the agreed headcount;
- make sure the project managers in the pool apply the company's approach to project management;
- prevent and resolve issues regarding the efficacy, supply or quality of project managers;
- recruit, retain/release, develop and reward the pool of project managers according to their performance;
- provide personal mentoring and support to project managers;
- provide training and education in the company's approach to project management.

Therefore, the head of project management should be authorized to:

- recruit and release project managers to satisfy current and forecast demand effectively;
- conduct annual appraisals and recommend rewards/penalties.

At the end of a year, the head of project management's performance should be assessed by:

- the extent to which demand for project managers has been met;
- how regularly the resource plan for project managers has been maintained;
- the extent to which project managers have achieved their targets.

What resource pool and matrix management allow are new ways of engaging the people who work in projects. Seeing projects as identifiable blocks of work, funded with a ring-fenced investment, means that they may be managed differently from BAU. Diverse teams from across the organization and beyond can be incentivized to work together to achieve shared project objectives in addition to their BAU targets.

Engage competent project managers

It may seem obvious from the Case study and that which has followed, but successful projects depend on effective sponsors *and* project managers. Working well, they work together. Allow sponsors the opportunity to select their own project manager; each will be the other's dependent.

Regardless of their present job title, identify a list of people who are, or have the potential to be, effective project managers (a further analysis of the competencies needed is covered in Chapter 8). Offer the list to your sponsors.

Tailor recruitment, induction and training

The Human Resource (HR) department must be made aware that, with a specific change management mindset growing in the business, there will be new skills to be sought from the marketplace. Specialist change management agencies may be engaged to support the HR department in this matter as traditional search and selection routes may be unsuitable.

Induction may be tuned for anyone joining the organization. In addition to discovering more about the operations of the organization they have joined, they may now learn of internal change management processes, projects which are underway, and the sponsors and project managers who lead them.

Training requirements may be considerable. Indeed, it is often the first tool which organizations new to change management will seize upon. However, it can also be a considerable investment and some thought is wise before committing swathes of people to a training programme. Here are some suggestions:

- Ensure that sponsors have been educated and briefed to a practical standard before training anyone else. Once familiar with the language of change management, and enthusiastic about their projects, they themselves will serve well to promote the mindset.
- You want your workforce to act as they have been trained, so ensure that the training is tailored to your organization's specific needs. Not only are you expecting them to gain new skills and knowledge, you are seeking a change in their attitude and behaviour. Ensure that your training provider understands this and helps to deliver it.
- Let change management specialists in your organization decide what training programme will suit the organization best. Don't leave the decision to a person or department that does not understand the subject matter.

Support, develop and educate the workforce

If it is not possible to find project management practitioners from inside your organization, be prepared to develop them to an effective standard. This may involve training, as described above. Alternatively or additionally, place them under the wing of a trusted sponsor or more senior project manager and let them gain experience on projects of ever-increasing complexity and risk. In this way, an organization *grows* its talent. And if this is not an option, recruit or buy in people with project management skills – it is a specialist and recognized discipline in which there are a great many contract practitioners. However, be advised that sponsorship cannot be found anywhere but inside the organization – do not be tempted to recruit a sponsor.

Do not disadvantage anyone working in a project for having been allocated to it. Be sure that they can continue to access all of the traditional routes for promotion should they seek them. Provide them in the usual way with a performance appraisal which takes account of the non-BAU work they have delivered. Perhaps compensate them for the losses they may incur from being taken away from their normal line of work.

From the top down, be sure to encourage everyone to believe in and apply the same fundamental principles. If any lack of confidence or discipline is displayed by senior management, it will not be in the least surprising if an identical culture grows beneath them.

Introduce and embed an approach to project management

A defined and clearly articulated approach to project management (or what is often called a methodology) is helpful since it describes the language of change which the organization has adopted. It is often a document which describes the processes, responsibilities and deliverables involved in the approach. However, one of the most common failings in the introduction of a change management mindset is the sole reliance on a methodology. It is only of real value when it is *applied*. The job of senior managers in a change-literate organization is to embed the practice and language such that they become second nature. Here are some suggestions as to how to develop and roll out an approach:

● Much like the approach to training, it is sensible to tailor the methodology according to the specific needs of the organization.

Indeed, it makes great sense to align the development of a training programme with the development of the methodology so that the language, principles and practices are consistent.

- Ensure that whoever is charged with authoring and delivering the approach is a seasoned, effective and respected project practitioner. The quickest way to lose all credibility is to produce a work which misunderstands or misrepresents the realities of working in a project environment.
- Create first a 'minimum standard' which can be quickly grasped and applied, and which needs the absolute minimum of maintenance. The more complex it is, the greater the policing needed to ensure compliance and the faster it will fall into disuse. Trial it on a few projects of different size, complexity and risk, then roll it out to the whole organization.
- Deliver incremental improvements no more frequently than every year. This will help to raise the bar gradually whilst allowing everyone to become familiar and comfortable with the standard.
- Reward compliance by demonstrating the benefits it has delivered to both the project and the organization. If people cannot see any advantage in something, they will not use it.

Invest in tools

The infrastructure of change management includes people, processes and, quite often, some tools. Given that the planning and reporting hierarchy for projects will be entirely different from that for the BAU organization structure, it may be helpful to invest in some tools which can aid in the planning, monitoring and control of projects. Amongst others, this will be covered in greater detail in Chapter 10.

Seek and measure the benefits

Why does any organization employ projects? The common justification is to ensure that, at some future point, the business can enjoy the rewards of change. If that ambition is to be realized, change must be measured. The BAU organization is familiar with progress measurement. Amongst many other metrics, it charts revenue growth and decline, cost control and profit fluctuation. Projects, in isolation and together as a portfolio, must be subjected to the same discipline. Any failure to do so will result in investment decisions which, at best, were ratified when the money was requested but which have not been vindicated since.

The argument for measuring the benefits within an individual project is an important but tired one. If organizations are persuaded that it is a good thing to do, they may have in place the necessary mechanics. If they are not yet fully change literate, it is likely that the maturity required to measure the benefits has not yet developed and that no one really knows whether a project was a sensible investment or not. Those organizations which do measure post-project benefits to judge the rewards often require the sponsor to stay in post long after the project has closed. It is they who do the measuring, and they who are rewarded or penalized, dependent on the eventual outcome.

But all that serves to encourage is the success of a single project. Whole organizations depend on a continuous portfolio of projects tripping off the production line, day in, day out. For the organization which is mature in its management of change, it must be possible to set, deliver and measure the benefits of the whole portfolio. This is complex and challenging, yet not impossible, and is a topic which will be explored in greater detail in the following chapter.

Conclusion

Alongside BAU, we might now add CAU – change as usual. Where the operation of the business was once considered the 'day job', it is now just as critical that change is considered a legitimate and essential part of it too. Embedding the culture needed to deliver successful change alongside the more traditional approach to BAU will take a long time, involve the commitment of almost everyone who works in the organization and cost money. Introducing the mindset required to deliver change will itself be a change for the organization. Furthermore, the pressure to *maintain* a focus on the practices outlined in this chapter and beyond must be relentless.

Introducing a new cultural attitude is a change in itself. In his book *Leading Change*, John Kotter wrote:

> *In the final analysis, change sticks when it becomes 'the way we do things around here', when it seeps into the bloodstream of the corporate body. Until new behaviours are rooted in social norms and shared values, they are subject to degradation as soon as the pressure for change is removed.*

He added that for any cultural change (such as I am describing in this book), there are several reasons why it may fail:

- There is no sense of urgency.
- A powerful, guiding coalition is not adequately created.
- The programme lacks a clear vision.
- The vision is poorly communicated.
- Essential change is prevented by a will to protect the status quo.
- Short-term wins are not systematically planned or delivered.
- Victory is declared too soon.
- Changes are not anchored in the organization's culture.

There is a case to be made for using a project to manage the introduction of the practices described in this book, not least to mitigate the risks above. For this reason, my final chapter shows how an organization might go about doing just that. But where would such a project feature amongst the many other priorities your organization wishes to pursue? The next chapter will consider the importance of prioritizing what matters most...

SUMMARY

- Changing the business is as much a part of the 'day job' as running it.
- The toolkit used to run the business is unsuited to governing projects.
- Without a sponsor and project manager working closely together, projects will descend into chaos.
- Organizations that engage a 'change mindset' will stand a greater chance of gaining a competitive advantage.
- In practice, the change mindset must be translated into many structural, procedural and cultural components, all of which are necessary if the business is to deliver strategic success through projects.

CHAPTER TWO

PRIORITIZE WHAT MATTERS MOST

This chapter covers:

- the challenges which will arise from failing to manage or communicate the priority of one project over another;
- the consequences for the whole institution when such failures remain unresolved;
- the ways in which organizations may better understand what changes they most need, which ones they can afford to deliver, and how the portfolio of projects may be tested to confirm its suitability.

The enthusiasm and goodwill of a workforce are resources from which every organization can benefit. Yet, like our pockets, the pots that contain them are not bottomless. When a deadline looms or when an unplanned demand arises, organizations can dip into this finite fund, using it to buy them out of a tight spot. But when progress is dependent on continued withdrawals and the pots themselves are not replenished sufficiently enough, the business will soon feel the consequences. Such behaviour is prevalent when organizations mistakenly believe that:

Myth 2: We can do everything we set our minds to.

In this chapter, we will understand how any organization must determine what it most needs to deliver with its limited resources.

CASE STUDY

A historic, private bank prided itself on its traditions of customer service and product excellence. But above all, *stability* was a key cultural and promotional benefit. Many of its high-worth customers had been clients of the bank for all of their lives. These were people who valued constancy; risk-taking and change were unpalatable to them. This client culture was, not unnaturally, reflected in the attitude of the bank and its workforce. It was a relatively safe and comfortable place.

However, with the global economic downturn, competitive pressures increased and costs had to be more assiduously controlled. Its former affluence had provided a contingency to muffle the impact of several failed projects. Any such safety net had since been removed. Not only was it now necessary to be more efficient in the delivery of essential incremental changes to the business, but larger innovations and efficiency initiatives had to be built into the schedule of work. The organization was unused to the ordered discipline needed to manage a portfolio of change activities. It was, however, well populated with committed and experienced workers who were prepared to invest of themselves. Their collegiate spirit created a great energy of which they were justly proud.

As a new year dawned, a set of objectives was presented for all to see. It identified a succession of ambitions which the business sought to meet in 12 months. Sponsors were assigned to each of its many strands. Enthusiasm was considerable. There were high-fives all round, quite inconsistent with its tradition.

Yet almost as soon as the year had begun, the business realized that it would have to lay off some people and be as productive as it had planned but with a reduced workforce. And as the months progressed, a series of regulatory changes required a flurry of new initiatives to be added to the list. But every time something new arrived, the senior management team persuaded those who remained to squeeze in 'just one more project'. The list of projects was becoming longer, pressures remained to reduce the headcount, and the pots of enthusiasm and goodwill were running low.

By the end of the year, the audit trail connecting the organization's objectives to the plan it needed to meet them had been all but lost. The changes which were achieved did little to advance the business's aspirations. Much had been begun which was either delayed or abandoned as workers became diverted by different priorities. Managers who shouted loudest had secured the scarcest resource to pursue what they believed were the priorities. Departments, such as IT, which sought to serve the whole business had retrenched into an independent list of priorities in an attempt to manage their own resource. These separate lists reflected less and less of the business's objectives, and managers had become more and more unwilling to commit their people to corporate initiatives for fear of failing to meet their own targets.

The bank lumbered into the next financial year, weaker and miserable. Its brand, which was perhaps its greatest asset, remained one of its few attractive features and served to secure a buyer who mercifully transformed the business with the introduction of a tightly governed programme of change, something which its former owners had been unable to do for themselves.

What this means

Achievability of vision

The organization's objectives had been set out in such a way as to serve best as a 'wish list'. Initially, this was inspirational, but as the list was completely unsupported by a plan to confirm what could be realistically achieved with the available resources, it latterly became no more than aspirational. Like the person who comes last in a game show, the organization was frustratingly teased to 'come and see what you could have won'.

Portfolio alignment

Not only would a plan have been able to determine the achievability of the objectives, it could have shown which projects would specifically deliver which strategic imperatives. As it was, there was no identified connection between the strategic objectives the organization sought, and the vehicles which were supposed to deliver them. Thus, the portfolio and the vision diverged. The business was being taken in a direction dictated by the projects it was undertaking, not by the vision it had set.

Priority management

Peter F Drucker, the distinguished American writer and management consultant said, 'Management is doing things right; leadership is doing the right things.'

There was an absence of change leadership. Had there been a managed alignment of the organization's projects to its objectives, priorities could have been identified and communicated more clearly, and greater control applied when there was pressure to change throughout the year. The business simply had no method for prioritizing – and re-prioritizing – the portfolio. This led to a loss of central control, and a retrenchment into what is commonly called 'silo management': decisions were taken with local, not corporate, interests at heart. That would not have been such a bad thing had those decisions been consistent with corporate priorities. But since priorities were, at best, 'fluid', resources were used inefficiently.

Resource management

In the absence of clear priorities, resource allocation became relatively arbitrary, being driven either by the dominance of one person's force of will over another or the fear of apocalyptic conse-quences. Typically, this meant that the board was being frequently pummelled with a succession of resource requests, clarifications and issues to which it had neither the time nor the expertise to adequately respond.

Nor had the board much room for manoeuvre. Without a ranked stack of projects or a contingency pot to fund further changes, it was left shuffling people from one crisis to another, further drawing on (and diminishing) the pot of goodwill.

Delivery management

Prioritization would have established which projects mattered most. Since the priorities were unclear, several projects which did deliver failed to contribute the volume or speed of return on investment desired by the business. So benefits were not being systematically delivered to fund future changes. Rather, they were producing posi-tive outcomes whenever they could and, given the constraints, these were neither as frequent nor as timely as needed.

Furthermore, the relatively randomized order in which projects were undertaken led to a confusion of interdependencies. Had any-one been able (which they were not!) to describe the connections between projects, the resulting map would have been both inde-cipherable and ever changing. Therefore, delays in one project had unforeseen consequences on another.

People management

There was a twofold impact on the engagement of the organization's people. Firstly, like their management team, they lost sight of the common objectives they had all sought to achieve a year earlier. The concept of corporate citizenship was destroyed. 'We're all in it together' became 'I hope I don't end up as deeply in it as you.' Secondly, they became exhausted by the apparently endless and changing list of initiatives which had to be delivered; in modern parlance, they were suffering from 'change fatigue'.

The contingency of the workforce's enthusiasm and goodwill had been drawn upon so heavily that it ran dry.

The consequences of ignoring the imperative

Many organizations set out with the ambition of pursuing every great idea they identified when they convened at the beginning of the year. But by failing to prioritize which initiatives matter most, they run out of money and deliver short.

In truth, they may have the expertise to do anything they set their minds to and the enthusiasm to complete it all, but the resources to do only a third. So the question is not so much about what they *can* do as what they *cannot*.

Driving a portfolio of projects to success is not just about an investment of determination or enthusiasm, but of concentrated resources. A great team may be able to deliver anything, but they are almost certainly not able to deliver everything. Demand nearly always outstrips supply.

Objectives are not delivered

When a portfolio is improperly managed, the objectives it was engaged to deliver are put at risk. Instead of transformation, nothing may change. Or a transformation may be achieved which was entirely undesirable, as suffered by the subject of the Case study. Either can be catastrophic.

People's efficiency and engagement are reduced

The greatest investment most organizations make is in their people. Businesses take time to plan the staff numbers and skills required to deliver BAU, but too few invest enough in managing their project resources to a similar standard. Without effective mechanisms in place to manage our human resourcing, not only will the well-being of our projects become compromised, but so too our people.

Customer service, product innovation and competitiveness are weakened

As described in the previous chapter, the consequences of mis-managing projects can be felt across – and beyond – the institution. As staff engagement is weakened and BAU is impacted, there is a knock-on effect on customer engagement. Product innovations are compromised, and competitiveness is damaged, exposing the organization's weaknesses to the will of the market.

The solutions

There is a rough but logical sequence to the order in which an organization might go about putting in place the solutions to overcome the challenges highlighted in this chapter. That it is rational is not to say it is without challenge. The greatest difficulty to be faced in such an undertaking is that of gaining the confidence and commitment of the business to adopt a new practice and language with which they are unfamiliar.

Let the business set its own priorities

All too often, the priorities of a business are constrained by the technical or operational strategies pursued by individual departments. When a specific function's voice is greater than the others, it can have the effect of unbalancing the organization's decision making. For the change agenda to be met, each department must have a voice in the debate, with the responsibility for arbitration being placed in the hands of a relatively impartial, but commercially-focused, mediator. Most organizations who are experienced in the delivery of change create a team to direct and manage the whole portfolio on behalf of the business. The concept of the Change Management Team (CMT) was introduced in the previous chapter.

The Change Management Team

The benefits of such a team can be significant:

- The board is freed from the tactical management of the portfolio in order that it may focus on the operation and development of the business.
- The varied and specialist interests of individual departments can be brought to bear on the portfolio so that it may be enriched.
- The change objectives sought by the business are supported by a selection of projects which are dynamically tailored to deliver them.
- The most efficient use is made of the resources available for pursuing the agenda for change.
- Mismatches in resource supply and demand can be identified before they compromise the organization.

The CMT's objective is to identify, prioritize, commission and deliver a balanced, value-rich mix of projects within a budget, aligned to the business's change objectives.

To achieve this it must:

- assist the board in the identification of candidate projects;
- commission business cases (the justifications for individual projects);
- (re-)prioritize the portfolio of projects throughout the year;
- apportion resources across the portfolio according to those priorities;
- identify and delegate ownership to suitable project sponsors;
- manage 'exceptions' where benefits are at risk, and report variances to the board;
- develop and authorize use of the organization's approach to project and change management.

The materials they need to assist them in their duties will include:

- an authorized and prioritized Project Register;
- an authorized portfolio of strategically aligned, resourced projects;

- a managed Summary Timescale Plan;
- a managed Resource/Budget Plan;
- a managed Change Control Log;
- a Portfolio Benefits Plan and Risk Register.

Its success may be measured in terms of the following questions:

- Do all participants carry the authority needed to make any decision required of them?
- Have participants been drawn from all areas from which decisions are needed?
- Are participants likely to remain committed to their responsibilities for the course of the CMT's operation?
- Is the mix of projects contributing to the achievement of defined business objectives as planned?
- Are commercial and strategic targets being met?
- Are projects within the portfolio being delivered on time and on budget?
- Are projects producing results of acceptable quality?
- Are resources across the portfolio being efficiently administered?
- Is change activity being balanced against the need to deliver BAU?

The actual mode of operation may be as follows:

- The board establishes its vision, strategy and success criteria for changes sought during the coming year.
- The cycle of change is aligned to any existing budgetary and planning cycle.
- The CMT interprets the business's objectives for change into proposed projects.
- Proposed projects are prioritized according to their own, and relative, importance.
- Successful proposals are initiated within the 'change budget' provided by the board.
- The CMT is chaired by an impartial but change-focused senior manager/director who can arbitrate and resolve disputes with authority.

- The CMT meets every month to:
  - identify/consider new candidate projects;
  - (re-)prioritize the projects in the portfolio;
  - commission Business Cases;
  - apportion resources across the portfolio;
  - identify suitable project sponsors;
  - delegate ownership of projects to project sponsors;
  - manage situations where benefits may be at risk;
  - approve closure of relevant projects.
- An executive is engaged to manage the day-to-day work between meetings.

The CMT is a body which the organization needs to believe is necessary. Without something like that described above, the value of any process, prioritization or resource management will have limited value. It is advisable that a body along the lines described is instituted. At its first meeting, it may be presented with an analysis of the present state...

Conduct a current state analysis

Nothing works better to persuade people of a stark solution than a stark problem. The entire debate, including matters such as where the organization is heading and what priorities it should pursue, can be initiated with a statement of the organization's resource supply and demand balance (or imbalance).

Figure 2.1 illustrates a comparison of the resources demanded by the entire portfolio, and the actual supply available to fund it. When populated with an organization's actual data, the dotted line shows the point up to which existing resources can be invested. In the example, the stack of projects above the line cannot be resourced unless there is additional funding or the stack is re-prioritized.

To create a real illustration of your own business's position requires a number of steps.

FIGURE 2.1

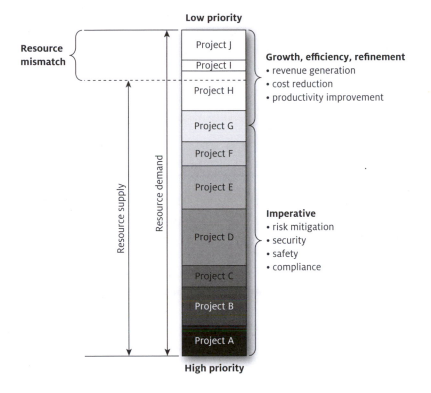

Describe what constitutes a 'project'

If a business is to manage its change agenda, as distinct from BAU, it must make absolutely clear what constitutes a 'project'. This requires more than only applying the worthy but general statement that it is:

● a temporary management environment created to produce a specified deliverable which, when used, leads to benefits which outweigh the investment made in its development and operation.

A set of simple criteria is needed by which to define which projects fall within the CMT's remit. Here is an example which may be refined according to your own organization's needs and scale:

● a piece of work requiring 15 or more days' effort, coordinated across more than one department.

The number of days specified is crucial. If it is set too high, the often enormous number of small projects which consume much – or most – of the resource could be excluded from the controls we are seeking to implement. Since such small initiatives can compromise the successful resourcing of larger projects, they should not be allowed to fall beneath the radar.

The criterion specifying *'more than one department'* is justified on the basis that the wider business can lose control of its resources when individual departments make direct and unauthorized demands on one another. For example, the IT resource in a business is finite, and must be responsibly managed to ensure that business priorities are met. Those institutional priorities can be compromised when departments divert IT resource to pursue non-critical or non-strategic activities.

However, the same criterion also allows for those same department managers to conduct discretionary projects with their *own* resources, providing they can fund them from their own budgets *and* still meet their obligations to the wider change agenda. For instance, the IT department will have a list of projects, such as software upgrades, which they will argue must be delivered without question for the business to continue to operate. There will be a case made that these do not qualify as corporate projects, since they involve only one department. If this is the case, then such work should be funded out of BAU. However, if an individual software upgrade is substantial enough that it requires other departments to be involved in, say, a training programme, there is a good case for treating it in the same way as any other of the organization's projects. That the IT department insists it is essential does not remove the obligation on them to justify it along with every other initiative that the organization is seeking to pursue.

It is well worth advertising these statements to the whole organization so that the criteria may not be misunderstood. Furthermore, there is value in adding that approved projects will be:

● commissioned to satisfy the organization's ability to conform to regulatory requirements, deliver strategic change and grow or refine itself;

- subject to formal governance to realize measurable operational or strategic benefit;
- assigned a sponsor and a cost code, without which they will not be considered legitimate.

Identify the projects

Compile a list of initiatives which qualify as projects according to the criteria noted above. Surprisingly, this is not as simple as it might first appear. It may soon be discovered that there are:

- mismatched expectations – one person's understanding of a project's objective or scope is different from another's;
- unidentified projects – projects about which little is known yet which are already underway and hungrily consuming resources;
- unformed projects – projects which have not yet been commissioned as they should;
- confused priorities – projects which have been incorrectly promoted or withheld;
- pet projects – projects which have the backing of an individual, but not of the business.

Record the projects

In seeking to resolve the problems identified above it is important to record the list of projects in a draft 'Project Register'. This will be of great importance as your organization grows to understand 'change'; the Project Register will come to represent the formal portfolio of initiatives which it employs to deliver its change agenda.

To begin with, a spreadsheet will be sufficient to contain some basic but essential information about each project, as shown in Figure 2.2.

The data which fills the Project Register describes something critical about each initiative which may well not have been clear beforehand. In truth, much may *remain* unclear, but at least there is now a basis upon which to construct a debate amongst those who have been charged with delivering the changes desired by the organization.

FIGURE 2.2

PROJECT REGISTER

PRIORITY	ID	PROJECT NAME	SPONSOR	COST CODE	START	END	*COST $
IMPERATIVE	A	Project A	Sponsor A	IMP0001	01/06/2011	30/09/2011	100,000
IMPERATIVE	B	Project B	Sponsor B	IMP0002	01/07/2011	31/03/2012	135,000
IMPERATIVE	C	Project C	Sponsor C	IMP0003	01/01/2012	28/02/2012	40,000
IMPERATIVE	D	Project D	Sponsor D	IMP0004	01/08/2011	31/05/2012	250,000
IMPERATIVE	E	Project E	Sponsor E	IMP0005	01/07/2011	31/10/2011	140,000
IMPERATIVE	F	Project F	Sponsor F	IMP0006	01/05/2012	31/08/2012	120,000
GROWTH	G	Project G	Sponsor G	GRO0001	01/10/2011	28/02/2012	150,000
GROWTH	H	Project H	Sponsor H		01/11/2011	31/05/2012	315,000
GROWTH	I	Project I	Sponsor I		01/09/2011	31/12/2011	80,000
GROWTH	J	Project J	Sponsor J		01/07/2011	31/08/2011	20,000
TOTAL							1,350,000

*assumes average monthly FTE rate of $5,000

At this time, the content of the Project Register is limited. As I will show through this and successive chapters, the data can be extended to assist in the effective management of the portfolio. For now, the most important fields are:

- Priority – is the project 'imperative' or not? For many projects, the answer will be anything but straightforward because different people will have different opinions. This is why it is so important to define explicitly what is meant by the term 'imperative'. It must be taken to mean that the project must happen in order to avoid business-threatening risk. Examples would include regulatory projects, the failure or delay of which would put the business in breach of its legal obligations. If the project is not imperative according to this definition, it falls into the Growth/Efficiency/Refinement category. This is taken to mean any other project for which a case can be made, but which is not imperative to the operation of the business. Crucially (and for this reason the subject of a whole chapter), every project must be cost-justified so that their relative merits and priority may be compared.
- Project name – to ensure that it is commonly recognized.
- Sponsor – as the previous chapter suggested, every project should be owned by a named individual within the organization who may be held accountable for its successful delivery. Without such, how will the entire portfolio be controlled?
- Cost code – no project should be authorized to commence unless it has been issued with a recognized, ring-fenced budget, indicated by the presence of a cost code.
- Start date – has the project begun? If so, it is probably already consuming resources and needs to be brought into the control of the portfolio.
- End date – at which point can the business expect the drain of project expense to end, and the accrual of benefits to begin?
- Cost – what specific burden is the project placing on the portfolio? This figure may be a financial value (ie its budget), or an expression of the 'person-day' or full-time equivalent (FTE) resource demanded by the project. Any will serve as long as they are applied consistently.

Identify the supply/demand mismatch

It is the figures in the 'Cost' column which, when added together, will equal the 'resource demand', one of the two crucial measures identified in Figure 2.1. The other which must be calculated is the 'resource supply' which is available to fund the change agenda. This may be a single figure which has been set aside by the board, or a value based on the total 'person-days' or FTEs available to the delivery of projects. Put another way, it is that resource which is *not* devoted to BAU.

When the 'resource demand' and 'resource supply' figures are compared, it will be possible, perhaps for the first time ever, to truly know the extent to which the two numbers are alike.

Figure 2.3 is a slightly more sophisticated illustration using some sample data which can be used to advance the debate.

FIGURE 2.3

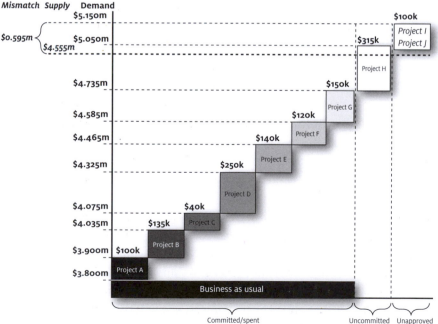

The business in question is faced with a resource demand of $5.150m to deliver its BAU obligations and its desired portfolio of projects, yet the budget available to cover both is $4.555m. Assuming the $3.8m set aside for BAU is not negotiable, the business faces a mismatch of $0.595m. So far, $0.935m has been committed to Projects A to G, with $0.415m (Projects H, I and J) remaining either uncommitted or unapproved.

This is typical of the challenges which will face the CMT. Yet in order to resolve the mismatch, a further, vital piece of information is missing. Effective prioritization cannot be based only on what the organization can *afford* to change. Of greater importance is taking account of what it *needs* to change if it is to meet its objectives. In the example, the business may either decide that Projects H, I and J will have to remain unachievable for now, find new money to fund them, or re-prioritize the whole register to rank them above something to which money has already been committed. The effective ranking requires that the CMT make a judgement based not only on the balance of supply and demand, but on what contribution each project will make to the advancement of the organization's change agenda.

Measure the alignment of the portfolio to the organization's objectives for change

It is possible to measure what contribution each project is making. This requires that the organization's change objectives are articulated in such a way as to allow this to happen.

Articulate the business's objectives

These may be contained in the Business Plan, or might have to be teased out from a range of other materials. Whatever the source or format, a series of statements is desirable which summarize the main content. Here is an example.

The organization will:

- retain its most important clients;
- bring in new clients;

- secure recurring revenues rather than one-off fees;
- further its alliance partnerships;
- deliver increased revenues;
- deliver increased margins;
- become number one in its marketplace;
- undertake short-term, high-yield projects;
- deliver a wider range of products;
- reduce its implementation timescales;
- reduce its implementation costs;
- deliver minimum maintenance products;
- engage in fixed-price or shared-risk initiatives;
- prioritize and justify every initiative it undertakes;
- have market-leading product quality and testing processes;
- employ cutting-edge product implementation processes;
- manage its projects using repeatable, proven principles and techniques;
- use new and innovative technologies;
- provide opportunities to help retain experienced staff;
- apply lessons that have been learned from experience;
- draw in and develop junior staff;
- increase the gap between itself and the competition.

This is a huge list and covers a vast scope. It may lack focus or fail to succeed in any number of ways, so it should be authenticated.

Validate the business's objectives

Before comparing projects to the list above, it is important that the set of objectives is validated.

The table in Figure 2.4 is a very simple and early example of the same objectives expressed as a 'balanced scorecard' of measures. The Balanced Scorecard, an approach developed by Robert Kaplan and David Norton, proposed a means by which to describe what strategic success could look like. An organization's targets and measures are described in four balanced quadrants: Commercial, Customer, Process and Learning.

A logic connects the four quadrants. Commercial success results from providing customers with what they want or need. The processes

FIGURE 2.4

Commercial objectives. *The organization will...*	Customer objectives. *The organization will...*
• retain its most important clients; • bring in new clients; • secure recurring revenues rather than one-off fees; • further its alliance partnerships; • deliver increased revenue; • deliver increased margins; • become number one in its marketplace; • undertake short-term, high-yield projects.	• deliver a wider range of products; • reduce its implementation timescales; • reduce its implementation costs; • deliver minimum maintenance products; • engage in fixed-price or shared-risk initiatives.
Process improvements. *The organization will...*	Learning and growth. *The organization will...*
• prioritize and justify every initiative it undertakes; • have market-leading product quality and testing processes; • employ cutting-edge product implementation processes; • manage its projects using repeatable, proven principles and techniques.	• use new and/or innovative technologies; • provide opportunities to help retain experienced staff; • apply lessons that have been learned from experience; • draw in and develop junior staff; • increase the gap between itself and the competition.

necessary to deliver those products and services must be efficient and effective. They become so by developing the organization's competencies, not least those of its people. The consideration of a business's aims and performance across the quadrants provides a means by which to judge how balanced they are.

Because the quadrants are linked by this logic, the list of statements needs to be checked for internal consistency. For instance, the laudable aim of engaging in fixed-price or shared-risk initiatives may not allow the delivery of increased margins. If the use of new and innovative technologies results in redundancies, how possible or desirable will it be to draw in and develop junior staff? Some objectives may be beyond the organization to control: the most important clients may decide not to buy the 'wider range of products'. Under such circumstances, what would matter most – client engagement or product leadership? If the statements are inconsistent, so too may be the business plan from which they were derived, and thus, so too will the portfolio of projects which eventually arises to satisfy it.

FIGURE 2.5

Project contribution to strategy	Projects		
Business objective	A	B	C
Will this project contribute to the organization securing $500,000 worth of recurring revenues during the coming year from clients that have always previously paid one-off payments?	Direct	Indirect	Absent
Will this project contribute to the organization delivering three implementations during the coming year in seven weeks rather than nine?	Absent	Absent	Absent
Will this project contribute to the organization implementing its own project management methodology during the coming year?	Indirect	Absent	Absent
Will this project contribute to the organization delivering two projects in the coming year using the new project management method?	Absent	Absent	Absent
Will this project contribute to the organization's reduction in the turnover of staff of more than 10 years' experience by 20% during the coming year?	Absent	Direct	Absent

Compare the portfolio to the business's objectives

The vertical axis of the Project Contribution Matrix in Figure 2.5 identifies just a small sample of statements from the original list where, normally, all would be included. The example statements have also been refined further to be measurable. The horizontal axis contains the names of the projects from the Project Register.

The intersections are where the contributions of projects to objectives are recorded. A project's contribution may be Direct, Indirect or Absent. In this way, the portfolio is compared to the strategy to determine whether the organization's change agenda is being supported by the projects it has underway. In the example above, some conclusions can be made, each of which must be addressed:

- No projects are contributing to the company delivering speedier implementations. Customers may become dissatisfied.
- Even if the company develops a new project management approach (and there is little evidence of this), no projects will use it.
- Project C is making no contribution to the company's strategic aims. Why is it being funded?

(Re-)Prioritize the projects

Upon presentation of an analysis such as that shown in Figures 2.3 and 2.5, the business (in the form of the CMT) is able to commence a more informed debate about its priorities. This may take a considerable time as everything will be open to challenge, including the estimates, the projects' names, their delivery dates and the way in which the importance of each project has been interpreted (Imperative, Growth/Efficiency/Refinement). Furthermore, new projects will be cropping up all the time, so the list will be shifting even as it is being debated.

An additional form of information to assist in such decision making is the Risk/Reward Matrix, as illustrated in Figure 2.6.

This enables each project to be considered in terms of its reward relative to the risk of its implementation.

The following statements are responded to with a 'yes' or 'no' for each project. Each 'yes' attracts a score of one point. The results are displayed on the matrix.

Rewards:
- The project is strategically imperative.
- This is a regulatory or legally mandated project.
- There is potential for long-term value creation.
- Perceived expected financial benefits are high.
- Expected value to customers is high.
- Expected value to employees is high.
- This project includes a 'wow' factor.

Risks:
- The project will present significant technical challenge.
- The project will require significant procedural change.
- The project will require significant organizational change.
- Implementation costs are expected to be high.
- The project cannot be implemented quickly.
- There is little appetite and/or capacity for this proposal.
- There will be significant impact on business as usual.

FIGURE 2.6

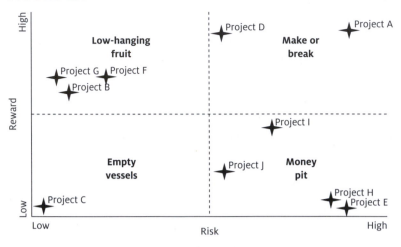

The four quadrants can be described as follows:

- Empty vessels – these may be pursued easily but may not deliver much reward. They may appear attractive because of their relative ease of implementation, but if they deliver little value, they will engage resources that could have been invested elsewhere.
- Money pit – projects that are high in risk and low in reward may appear unpalatable, but they may be necessary. Like empty vessels, they deserve debate to avoid the danger of their being discounted merely because of their risk profile. Examples may include regulatory or mandatory projects where the only benefit is risk avoidance.
- Low-hanging fruit – these are preferable to empty vessels. Not only are they relatively low-risk projects, but they also appear to promise high rewards.
- Make or break – projects in this category will be those of which most people in the organization already have some awareness. They will be controversial and challenging and may divide opinion. They will make or break the portfolio, the department or even the entire business. If any projects in the portfolio deserve further and full examination of their costs and benefits, it is these.

The resulting picture does not provide a definitive perspective, but offers a further view of the portfolio which can support the CMT and others in the conclusions they draw.

Communicate the priorities and (re-)allocate resources

As the shape of the portfolio becomes clearer, it will be crucial to clearly and authoritatively communicate the consequences. This may involve the re-allocation of resources from one project to another, the postponement or cancellation of others, and the commissioning of new ones, all of which will have a considerable impact on the workforce's understanding, focus and motivation.

The outcome of a communication and realignment such as has been described must ensure that, henceforth:

- All project activity is aligned to the business's objectives.
- All projects are funded within the constraints of the available budget.
- The designated list of projects and priorities carries the authority of the board.

Steer the portfolio to meet its objectives within agreed constraints

Such governance requires continued management. For instance, the continued balance of resource supply and demand must be maintained, and the complex interdependence of shifting projects must be controlled. Arguably of greater importance is the need to ensure that the portfolio continues to take the business in the direction of its targets for change.

There are various tools to support the CMT in doing all of this, which are refinements or embellishments of those already discussed.

Balance resource supply and demand

Figure 2.7 shows how the Project Register may be developed to identify the monthly resource demand, supply and mismatch, so that the ever-changing picture may be managed.

Manage the interdependence of projects

Figure 2.8 illustrates the key interdependencies so that the consequence of delays might be understood. Each arrow is explained by some text denoting the nature of the dependence, but it is quite common practice to develop a simple 'dependency agreement' between the two bodies (projects or organizations) to serve as a form of contract between them.

Balance the contribution of projects to the business's change objectives

Figure 2.9 shows how the data captured in the fully populated Project Contribution Matrix might be translated into a graphical representation. In this way, the business is able to know how the projects it has selected to advance the change agenda actually contribute across the four Balanced Scorecard quadrants. That it seems to be uneven does not automatically signify a problem; the picture painted is merely one further piece of management information which may be used to make informed decisions about which projects to promote. However, if the picture were to remain unbalanced year after year, there may be cause for concern that some areas were not receiving sufficient investment.

Conclusion

Steps to scope and define the portfolio have been taken. The business has:

- a clearer set of objectives for change;
- an identified, authorized, funded and prioritized portfolio;
- a focused and, hopefully, motivated workforce.

And the risk of failure will have been reduced, which is a positive outcome. However, it is also important to paint a *realistic* assessment of what such governance means. The business will spend more time than ever trying to understand and articulate what it originally thought was a simple strategy. It will spend more time telling people why they can't start their projects than why they can, but its arguments will be better informed. Elation will be replaced by pragmatism. More of what the organization set out to do will be achieved and will be better aligned to strategic imperatives.

So, the portfolio has been described, justified and authorized. All that remains is to delegate the job of delivering it...

FIGURE 2.7

PROJECT REGISTER

PRIORITY	ID	PROJECT NAME	SPONSOR	COST CODE	START	END	*COST $	Jun	Jul	Aug	Sep	Oct	Nov	Dec	Jan	Feb	Mar	Apr	May	Jun	Jul	Aug	Sep	Oct	Nov	Dec
IMPERATIVE	A	Project A	Sponsor A	IMP0001	01/06/2011	30/09/2011	100,000	5	5	5	5															
IMPERATIVE	B	Project B	Sponsor B	IMP0002	01/07/2011	31/03/2012	135,000		3	3	3	3	3	3	3	3	3									
IMPERATIVE	C	Project C	Sponsor C	IMP0003	01/01/2012	28/02/2012	40,000								4	4										
IMPERATIVE	D	Project D	Sponsor D	IMP0004	01/08/2011	31/05/2012	250,000			5	5	5	5	5	5	5	5	5	5							
IMPERATIVE	E	Project E	Sponsor E	IMP0005	01/07/2011	31/10/2011	140,000		7	7	7	7														
IMPERATIVE	F	Project F	Sponsor F	IMP0006	01/05/2012	31/08/2012	120,000												6	6	6	6				
GROWTH	G	Project G	Sponsor G	GRO0001	01/10/2011	28/02/2012	150,000					6	6	6	6	6										
GROWTH	H	Project H	Sponsor H		01/11/2011	31/05/2012	315,000						9	9	9	9	9	9	9							
GROWTH	I	Project I	Sponsor I		01/09/2011	31/12/2011	80,000				4	4	4	4												
GROWTH	J	Project J	Sponsor J		01/07/2011	31/08/2011	20,000		2	2																
TOTAL							1,350,000																			

BUSINESS OUTCOMES

- All Sponsors trained
- New product available for customers
- Staff gymnasium
- All personal reviews complete
- Cafeteria redecorated
- Project Management approach mandated
- Backup space doubled
- Top floor available for use
- Recurring revenues commence from BigCorp deal
- Print software compliant

Resource Demand (FTEs)

RESOURCE DEMAND (FTEs)	*COST $	Jun	Jul	Aug	Sep	Oct	Nov	Dec	Jan	Feb	Mar	Apr	May	Jun	Jul	Aug	Sep	Oct	Nov	Dec
IMPERATIVE	785,000	5.0	15.0	20.0	20.0	15.0	8.0	8.0	12.0	12.0	8.0	5.0	11.0	6.0	6.0	6.0	0.0	0.0	0.0	0.0
GROWTH	565,000	0.0	2.0	2.0	4.0	10.0	19.0	19.0	15.0	15.0	9.0	9.0	9.0	0.0	0.0	0.0	0.0	0.0	0.0	0.0
BAU	3,800,000	40.0	40.0	40.0	40.0	40.0	40.0	40.0	40.0	40.0	40.0	40.0	40.0	40.0	40.0	40.0	40.0	40.0	40.0	40.0
TOTAL	5,150,000	45.0	57.0	62.0	64.0	65.0	67.0	67.0	67.0	67.0	57.0	54.0	60.0	46.0	46.0	46.0	40.0	40.0	40.0	40.0

Resource Supply (FTEs)

RESOURCE SUPPLY (FTEs)	*BUDGET $	Jun	Jul	Aug	Sep	Oct	Nov	Dec	Jan	Feb	Mar	Apr	May	Jun	Jul	Aug	Sep	Oct	Nov	Dec
Permanent	2,850,000	30.0	30.0	30.0	30.0	30.0	30.0	30.0	30.0	30.0	30.0	30.0	30.0	30.0	30.0	30.0	30.0	30.0	30.0	30.0
Temporary	902,500	9.5	9.5	9.5	9.5	9.5	9.5	9.5	9.5	9.5	9.5	9.5	9.5	9.5	9.5	9.5	9.5	9.5	9.5	9.5
Contract	802,500	7.0	7.0	7.0	8.5	8.5	8.5	9.0	9.0	10.0	10.0	10.0	10.0	11.0	11.0	11.0	11.0	5.0	5.0	2.0
TOTAL	4,555,000	46.5	46.5	46.5	48.0	48.0	48.0	48.5	48.5	49.5	49.5	49.5	49.5	50.5	50.5	50.5	50.5	44.5	44.5	41.5

Variance (FTEs)

VARIANCE (FTEs)	$	Jun	Jul	Aug	Sep	Oct	Nov	Dec	Jan	Feb	Mar	Apr	May	Jun	Jul	Aug	Sep	Oct	Nov	Dec
TOTAL	−595,000	1.5	−10.5	−15.5	−16.0	−17.0	−19.0	−18.5	−18.5	−17.5	−7.5	−4.5	−10.5	4.5	4.5	4.5	10.5	4.5	4.5	1.5

*assumes average monthly FTE rate of $5,000

FIGURE 2.8

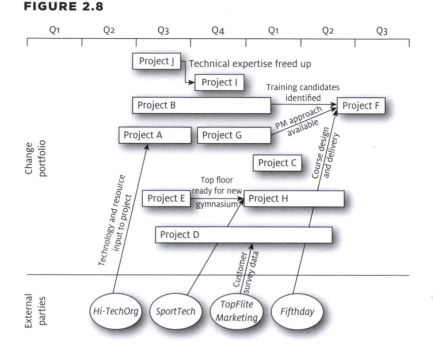

FIGURE 2.9

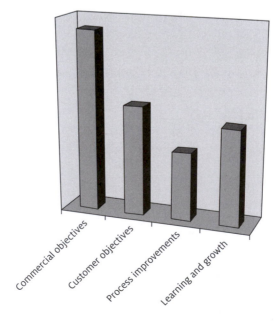

SUMMARY

- Allow the business to identify and set its own priorities for change.
- Devolve responsibility for the governance of the organization's change agenda to a Change Management Team, so as not to divert the board.
- Secure the participation and commitment of every part of the business.
- Calculate the costs of the existing portfolio and compare it to the available supply in order that mismatches may be determined and managed.
- Decompose the organization's objectives for change into measurable statements so that they may be verified as internally consistent and suitably balanced.
- Identify the contribution each project is making towards the achievement of the organization's change agenda in order that the portfolio can be used to move the organization in the intended direction.
- Communicate the consequences of any resourcing or priority changes clearly and authoritatively to the whole organization to ensure focus, understanding and motivation are maintained.
- Maintain direction and pace by controlling the priorities and resourcing for change.

CHAPTER THREE

DELEGATE, BUT DO NOT ABDICATE, RESPONSIBILITY

This chapter covers:

- the challenges which will arise from failing to clearly define responsibilities amongst the participants involved in any project activity;
- the consequences for the whole institution when such failures remain unresolved;
- the ways in which organizations may better structure and empower those people who are to be engaged in the commissioning, management and delivery of projects.

No one doubts that the contribution of a competent project manager can be transforming. They can interpret the project's objective into a series of steps. They can motivate the team. They can control progress. They can deliver what was asked of them. From chaos, they can create order. Yet it is not at all unusual that organizations come to assume very much more of them, leading to the false expectation that:

Myth 3: A great project manager will bring success.

In this chapter, we will discover that the project manager is not the only, nor the most important, person involved in the project, and that successful change depends upon a clear separation and distribution of responsibility and authority across a wide variety of stakeholders.

CASE STUDY

The sales director of an international manufacturing business was insistent that he be allowed to introduce a widely available customer relationship management (CRM) software package for all sales teams across the world. The company's more effectively coordinated rivals were known to have it and he felt strongly that, without the consistency of approach and greater focus it would engender, regional sales teams would be less able to identify and develop global opportunities. Having sought to persuade his contemporaries on the senior management team at every opportunity that the project would result in higher-value, worldwide deals, approval was eventually given. Euphoric at the decision, he sought and found a project manager to whom he handed over responsibility for delivery. The machinery of change shifted up a gear as work began to install the software package.

During the seven months it took to do so, the sales director was not to be seen as his BAU obligations drove him to spend all of his time with the company's clients. Besides, he had achieved his objective in securing approval for the solution and had found someone to implement it. The project was in a safe pair of hands; his work was done. He could find no motivation to play a continued role in the initiative.

The project manager had inherited a clear instruction: implement the software. However, the practice was not without challenge. Since a named software package had been specified, there was little leeway to accommodate unique, regional requirements, but that did not stop the regions from trying. Where refinements were possible, the project manager found herself having to broker agreements across the world to ensure that the solution was agreeable to everyone, and where it was not, she had to arbitrate. And it was soon discovered that the package would only interface with the organization's diary and e-mail system if a significant, additional financial investment were to be made. The project manager had no power to authorize any further expenditure and no one to turn to for a solution, so the lack of an interface remained.

Nevertheless, the project surged onwards, driven by the project manager's tenacity and a commitment to the plan. As the time came to complete the initiative, a specialist trainer travelled widely to ensure that every user knew how the system worked, and how they should use it. Thereafter, there was little more for the project manager or her team to do, short of making the software available to every salesperson.

The software package was implemented within its operating constraints on the day predicted by the project manager seven months previously. Account was taken of the last remaining invoices to be submitted, and the project was considered to have been completed according to budgetary estimates. By the measure of many respected and professional institutions, it had been a success. Certainly, the project manager considered it so, for despite the hitches, the package was implemented as she had forecast in the plan. Furthermore, she had maintained morale in the team, identified many risks which were managed in advance, and controlled the inevitable changes which occurred during the project. In the absence of a supportive body above her, she had done as much as her authority allowed. Much more could not have been expected. A few days after implementation, she moved on to her next project.

Some years later, in what had become a chastened and demanding economic environment, I had cause to visit the organization. I asked a member of the board to what extent the CRM system had contributed to their aspiration for more numerous global sales deals. My query was greeted with a weariness and embarrassment born of having been tormented with the same question many times before. An attachment to the local systems previously used by each region had underpinned their failure to adopt the new package. The investment in the CRM system, sponsored by the sales director, had failed to achieve the proposed benefits. Competitors continued to identify, develop and deliver the big, global deals. The board considered the project an abject failure. From their perspective the investment in what became an unused system represented a waste of precious resource which might have been used more profitably elsewhere.

Ironically, the organization's eventual reaction took little account of its previous failures. A new sales director was in position, developing a case for an alternative CRM solution which, he asserted, would overcome the technical shortfalls of the original. The business was about to embark on an almost identical project, face almost identical problems and, probably, deal with them in an almost identical fashion.

What this means

It takes an organization to deliver a project

The Case study illustrates that the faults within the project were few and minor compared with those outside it. Whether or not the project was well managed matters less than how it came to be endorsed. The previous chapter considered the importance of a commissioning and control body to oversee the portfolio: the Change Management Team (CMT). The obligations expected of such a body were clearly unapparent; the board demonstrated their unsuitability to operate in place of a CMT. So perhaps the project should have never begun, or should have been subject to greater control in its commissioning. However, the greater fault lies with the inexperience of the sponsor. He considered his role to have ended when the decision was made to award funds to the project. In point of fact, it was just at that time that his involvement in the project should have increased. As described in Chapter 2, the sponsor applied his BAU mindset to the management of change, and fell at the first hurdle.

The failure of the project may also be attributed to the sales teams around the world who failed to endorse and use the system presented to them. It was only upon their adoption of it that any benefit was likely to arise.

And what of the technicians? Could they not have advised in advance that the selected package would not interface sufficiently well with the company's systems suite? They were only offered the opportunity to invest their energy, not their expertise, so it is hardly remarkable that the problem remained unforeseen until it was too late to overcome economically.

Together, everyone caused the project to flop but, as we will explore, some made a greater contribution to its failure than others.

Accountability, authority and responsibility become confused

When the board approved the expenditure, they delegated the responsibility for delivery of the proposed benefits to the sales director. Yet in doing so, they remained (as a board) accountable for the endeavour since it was they who had made the investment decision, and it was they who would wish to see the benefits measured in increased revenues and profits.

Their hopes of the sales director were not misplaced because he had the authority to meet their expectations. However, he did not have the interest. He believed that, in securing the services of a project manager, his obligations to the project had been satisfied. This was far from the case. In delegating responsibility for the delivery of the project, he was not delegating his authority, nor his accountability, nor the responsibilities that only he could discharge. He remained the senior-most individual within the project; that he placed himself firmly outside it did not remove his liability.

The character at the bottom of this management food chain was the project manager. She inherited responsibility for implementing the CRM solution on time, on budget and to specification. The authority vested in her as a project manager afforded her the power to work within some reasonably specific boundaries. For example, she could spend money which had been approved for the project, but could not authorize the additional investment needed for the missing interface – only the sales director could do so. So any expectations that her involvement would deliver more than an implemented system and some trained users were misplaced.

Because accountabilities, authority and responsibilities were completely confused, the *power* to deliver true success was progressively dissipated as the project was delegated further and further down the line.

Another global business, not unlike that outlined in the Case study, experienced a similar problem, although it was manifested differently. Their board accepted the concept of identified sponsors being held accountable for delivering the project's benefits. Yet when those same sponsors sought to use some of their allotted budget to engage external resources to populate their teams, the board prevented them from doing so, citing their preference to avoid contract resource. So the board delegated responsibility, but not the commensurate authority, and effectively rendered the sponsors impotent.

Sponsors deliver change, not products

It is not at all uncommon for sponsors to misunderstand their responsibilities, yet the consequences of doing so can be dire, leading not only to project, but enterprise-wide failures. As noted above, the absence of a committed sponsor partly resulted in an absence of some key obligations. Some crucial things did not happen because there was no one present to worry about them.

For instance, the system was successfully implemented, at which point the project manager's principal responsibilities were complete. Yet no one remained engaged and committed who could embed, or be held accountable for embedding, the post-project benefits. The salespeople around the world can hardly be blamed for their reluctance to adopt the system: they had been trained to use it but not *persuaded*. In this respect, the sponsor might have made the difference between *true* success and failure, motivating the sales workforce to embrace the change rather than reject it.

Sponsorship is more about leadership than management

It is true to say that leadership is a characteristic which is desirable in a project manager. But project managers need to take their instruction from someone too; they and the project need a leader. The sales director succeeded in commissioning the project, but failed to provide the motivation, direction setting and power which were needed continuously. The drive and ambition required by any change initiative were missing.

Whenever any member of a busy team (including the project manager) looks up from their work, they should see the sponsor above and ahead of them.

Successful relationships are at the heart of effective sponsorship

The sales director formed and used relationships to advance his personal and BAU objectives, but not those of the project. In fact, once the initiative had begun, he had no relationship at all with the project or any of its stakeholders.

There were several relationships which he failed to form. First and foremost, he should have invested his time and energy into engaging with the project manager. It was through that individual that he maintained access to the project. In this way, he would have known more about the project and could have reacted effectively through the project manager when necessary.

Secondly, he formed no relationships with the body of users on whom he was seeking to impose the solution he had selected for them. And thirdly, he failed to engage sufficiently enough with those technicians on whose skills and expertise the project would depend.

No one knows everything

The sponsor considered himself sufficiently competent not only to make the case for the financial investment, but also to speak on behalf of those who would use the system, and those who would have been best placed to propose a solution. Since he was actually qualified to do only the first of these three things, the decisions made in the latter two were ill informed and unauthoritative.

The consequences of ignoring the imperative

Responsibilities become confused

As responsibilities become confused, so do roles. As this happens, people misunderstand or forget what is expected of them and revert to the line role in which they may have greater comfort, confidence or knowledge. Within projects, essential activities are not carried out, decisions cannot be made and the efficiency of the 'change machine' is much reduced.

Responsibilities, and the authority needed to discharge them, become incompatible

As responsibilities are delegated too far down the management hierarchy, the authority to discharge them is lost, rendering the manager powerless to act. Too much becomes expected of the project manager. They become less able to focus on the purpose for which they have been recruited. The value they contribute to the organization is reduced and, if they leave the organization, lost altogether.

The change portfolio becomes impossible to steer

With no one to promote the vision for each initiative, the course of each project within the portfolio diverges from the wider agenda, resulting in a failure to change the business as expected. Furthermore, with inappropriate or ineffectual people at the helm of each project, there are few means by which the governing bodies may effect corrections.

At best, projects deliver products, but not benefits

With luck, tenacity and resolve, a project manager alone can succeed in delivering a product from the project. Whether it will be adopted by the user community, have a sufficiently robust build quality to work, or deliver any benefits, are beyond their control and authority to affect.

The solutions

Engage accountable, authoritative sponsors

What precisely is expected of a sponsor? If this is better understood, it may be easier to select one. Here is a role description:

Role purpose:

- to deliver a commercially viable outcome;
- to assume ownership of the project on behalf of the Change Management Team.

Benefits of role:

- Allows the Change Management Team to delegate responsibility for the delivery of a package of benefits to a named and accountable individual, thereby allowing them to maintain control of the wider portfolio.
- Allows for an emphasis to be placed on the delivery of benefits, rather than on time, cost and quality expectations alone.
- Provides an opportunity to inject a sense of leadership into the project.
- Allows for the alignment of project and business objectives, thereby ensuring the project remains both viable and relevant.
- Allows for changes in business strategy to be interpreted such that the project may change direction if necessary.

Responsibilities:

- to own the Business Case on behalf of the Change Management Team, ensure that it is maintained, and deliver the commercial benefits it promises;

- to brief the Change Management Team about project progress, escalating when outside agreed benefit escalation conditions;
- to translate strategic or commercial matters and brief relevant stakeholders such that well-informed decisions may be taken;
- to authorize the commencement of the project;
- to authorize the plan and agree expenditure;
- to resolve any priority or resource conflicts through arbitration with user and specialist Project Steering Group members;
- to organize and chair Project Steering Group meetings;
- to set escalation conditions for the Project Manager;
- to authorize action if escalation conditions are forecast to be breached;
- to authorize the closure of the project, on agreement with other Project Steering Group participants;
- to report the realization of benefits to the Change Management Team in accordance with the agreed realization timetable.

Reporting to:

- Change Management Team.

Reporting from:

- other Project Steering Group members;
- Project Manager.

Deliverables:

- approved and maintained Business Case (the project's justification);
- Lessons Learned Report;
- Benefits Realization Report.

Measures of success:

- The Business Case remains current at all times.
- The commercial and strategic benefits identified in the Business Case are delivered according to the timetable.
- The Project Manager remains suitably briefed at all times.
- A suitable Project Steering Group is in place throughout the life of the project.

- A suitable level and form of governance is used to manage the project.
- That which is delivered by the project is in accordance with the expectations of the Change Management Team.

But as the role requires considerable leadership skills, it is just as important to identify the competencies required of any selected individual:

Desirable skills (a sponsor's ability to do what is required of them):

- envisioning (defining and describing what success looks like);
- articulating and quantifying benefits;
- stakeholder management and networking;
- risk identification and management;
- negotiation;
- delegation;
- conflict management;
- arbitration;
- people management;
- communication;
- ability to sell ideas and concepts;
- motivational;
- influencing;
- team identification and development.

Desirable knowledge (a sponsor's possession of relevant information and facts):

- the organization's approach to change and project management;
- the organization's business strategy and approach;
- the area of business in question;
- relevant business products and services;

- processes and computer applications related to the area in question;
- technical or build standards relating to the key business deliverable;
- project commissioning, approval and initiation processes;
- planning and management of benefits;
- project financial management;
- risk management;
- stakeholder management;
- project planning (in order to engage practically with the Project Manager).

Desirable experience (a sponsor's involvement in, or exposure to, relevant past events and activities that have a bearing on the project or their role):

- sponsorship of other (ideally similar) projects;
- evidence or demonstration of competencies identified above;
- project and change management;
- management of people and teams;
- management in a matrix environment;
- delegation of work;
- Business Case compilation and promotion;
- benefits management;
- stakeholder management;
- risk management, possibly from an operational perspective;
- negotiation, especially with external parties;
- arbitration and conflict resolution;
- use of approach to project and change management.

Desirable characteristics (the personal attributes which a sponsor should possess in order to be able to discharge their responsibilities to the project):

- approachable;
- challenging;
- organized;
- self-motivated;
- motivational;

- problem solving;
- creative;
- inspirational;
- influential and persuasive;
- confident;
- professional;
- available;
- supportive;
- demonstrably accountable.

It would be unusual to find someone who exactly matches the outline described above. If such a person *does* exist in an organization, they are likely to be already engaged in the sponsorship of projects. However, not only is it not always possible to identify the perfect candidate, it is also unnecessary; a sponsor's competence will grow as they develop by doing the role. There are several ways by which an organization can support their development:

- Assign a mentor or buddy to provide support throughout their engagement.
- Invest in their education – there are many events, courses and development programmes suited to those involved in senior change management positions.
- Involve them as participants in projects sponsored by someone else so that they may see effective sponsorship in action.
- Identify them earlier than needed, and assign them to smaller or less risky initiatives such that they may be able to perform at an increased level when the time comes.

Individuals suited to the role must bear not only a good proportion of the competencies described above, but also the authority to act as the senior-most participant in the project. If a selected candidate does not have the organization's delegated authority to discharge their role, they should be granted it, if only for the duration of the project. In any case, suitable candidates are likely to be found in the more senior echelons of the organization. When the CMT identifies a potential candidate for the role of sponsor in one of the organization's projects, they should take care to ensure the individual is not so senior as to be too distant from it, and not so disconnected from the subject matter as to be disinterested. To put the point in modern parlance, the individual needs 'some skin in the game', for without it, their motivation to deliver a truly successful outcome will be dissipated by other pressures.

There is benefit to be gained from a formal or structured selection process. The requirement to participate in an interview or presentation can serve not only to test the potential candidates' mettle, but also to ensure there is a clear understanding between them and the commissioning body (the CMT). And at such a time, it would be both possible and sensible to negotiate the rewards available to the sponsor on successful delivery of the benefits. These may include promotional prospects, bonus payments or the promise of similar, engaging work. In any case, the reward must be linked to a defined and measurable outcome, more discussion of which will be covered in future chapters.

Practise balanced decision making

No matter how qualified or effective in the role the selected candidate may be, they will view the project from a very specific perspective. As sponsor, their principal obligation is to deliver a commercially viable outcome. They may pursue this imperative to the possible exclusion of other, competing and relevant points of view. For project sponsorship to be successful throughout the life of the project and beyond, a balanced approach to crucial decision making is essential.

Throughout the life of a project, decisions will be taken which affect its progress. It is helpful if these decisions are taken with the benefit of insight from the different interest groups in the project. These groups may be diverse and possibly antagonistic. However, healthy decisions are best made when varied perspectives can be brought to bear on the question. In a project, there are three distinct interests which it is essential to engage and protect (see Figure 3.1).

FIGURE 3.1

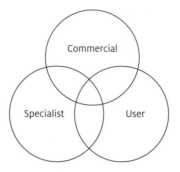

There will be people who have an interest in seeing the project achieve the commercial targets it has been set. They may have invested in it or wish to benefit from the improvements it will ultimately deliver. This perspective is represented by the sponsor, to which end they must have the competencies and authority described above. The Case study's sales director was a candidate for this role, yet he had not been sufficiently motivated to continue his interest in the project beyond its commissioning.

There are those who will wish to know that the project's output is fit for its intended purpose, because they will be required to use or operate it. In the Case study, this was the community of salespeople whose failure to adopt the solution resulted in a failure of the sponsor to achieve the advertised benefits.

And there are those who will be keen to ensure that the project's deliverables have been developed and built by competent specialists who understand, and have conformed to, appropriate policies and procedures. It is the absence of this body of expertise and authority in the Case study that led to the failure to identify the missing interface.

In practice, one of the most effective ways of drawing together these three interests is for the sponsor to build a senior project management team to complement the sponsor's authority and extend their ability to make insightful and well-informed decisions. This body of people is commonly called the Project Steering Group. It is such bodies to whom ownership of the project is passed by the CMT in order that the change aspirations of the business may be realized through effective direction.

FIGURE 3.2

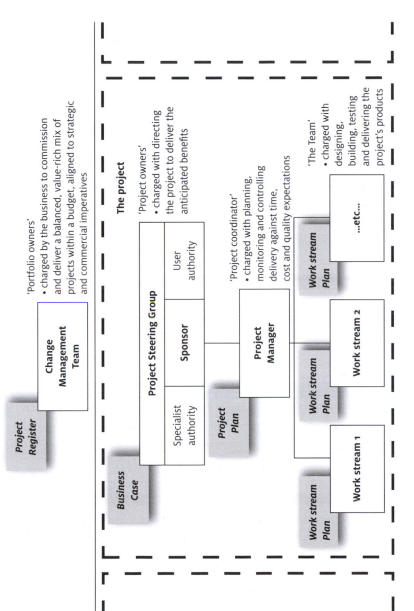

Project Register

Change Management Team

'Portfolio owners'
• charged by the business to commission and deliver a balanced, value-rich mix of projects within a budget, aligned to strategic and commercial imperatives

The project

Business Case

Project Steering Group

| Specialist authority | Sponsor | User authority |

'Project owners'
• charged with directing the project to deliver the anticipated benefits

Project Plan

Project Manager

'Project coordinator'
• charged with planning, monitoring and controlling delivery against time, cost and quality expectations

Work stream Plan — Work stream 1

Work stream Plan — Work stream 2

Work stream Plan — ...etc...

'The Team'
• charged with designing, building, testing and delivering the project's products

Figure 3.2 illustrates the hierarchy of authority in and around the project. The Project Steering Group, when tailored to accommodate the needs of the business, project and workforce, may serve as its senior management team. Above them is the CMT from whom their instructions are received and to whom the benefits are delivered. Beneath them is the Project Manager who must deliver the project's deliverable according to the method described in the plan.

The user interests, described above, are represented and protected by a User authority. The interests of those who are accountable for designing and building the solution to the users' needs are represented by a Specialist authority. Thus, with the sponsor at the helm, protecting and acting on behalf of the project's commercial investors, the project has the body of authoritative expertise it needs to describe, promote and deliver its vision. Here is a role outline for this crucial body:

Role purpose:

- to deliver the expectations described in the Business Case.

Benefits of role:

- Those with varied and critical interests in the success of the project are provided with an opportunity to contribute to its progress.
- Decisions which are beyond the authority of the Project Manager may be taken by named, accountable individuals.
- Decision making is made more effective and efficient due to the careful pre-selection of participants most suited to the Project Steering Group.
- True project success is placed in the hands of those who most want to see it delivered.
- Direction can be provided to the Project Manager, who might otherwise not understand the project's imperatives.

Responsibilities:

- to develop a Business Case that describes the project's entire (not just commercial) expectations for success;
- to confirm responsibilities and objectives with the Project Manager;
- to approve the plan, organization structure and controls;
- to agree escalation conditions with the Change Management Team above and the Project Manager beneath;
- to secure and commit project resources required by the project plan;
- to provide guidance and direction to the project, ensuring it remains within any specified constraints;
- to review each completed stage and approve progress to the next;
- to take responsibility for the mitigation of any risks which fall outside the control of the Project Manager;
- to decide upon any changes which are outside the Project Manager's control;
- to seek resolution of any issues that are outside the remit of the Project Manager;
- to comply with directives from the Change Management Team;
- to assure themselves that all products have been delivered satisfactorily;
- to provide assurance to others that all success criteria have been met;
- to authorize the closure of the project;
- to recommend any follow-on actions and the passage of these to the appropriate authorities;
- to arrange, where appropriate, for a Benefits Review to confirm that the intended commercial outcome was achieved;
- to inform the Change Management Team of all project closure decisions.

Reporting to:

- Change Management Team.

Reporting from:

- Project Manager.

Deliverables:

- approved Business Case;
- approved Requirements Specification (authorized by the User authority);
- approved Solution Design (authorized by the Specialist authority);
- approved Organization, Roles and Responsibilities;
- approved Project Plan.

Measures of success:

- the extent to which the Business Case is maintained, is always accessible, and illustrates the difference between the company's total effort or investment in the project compared with the income or benefit from it;
- the extent to which the project produces a value-adding outcome as identified in the Business Case;
- the extent to which the group has identified and empowered a single Project Manager to plan, coordinate and control the project;
- the extent to which they have been able to set and apply escalation conditions for the Project Manager;
- the extent to which they have applied 'management by exception', where the group is immediately informed by the Project Manager if forecast timings and costs are outside agreed escalation conditions;
- the extent to which they have been able to provide sufficient resources of the necessary quality to allow the plan to be fulfilled.

Considering the User authority, the role may be defined as follows:

Role purpose:

- To ensure the user expectations of the project are specified and delivered.

Benefits of role:

- The needs of the users are given a profile, increasing the likelihood that the project's deliverable will meet their expectations.
- Change Requests can be promoted or challenged by a champion, increasing the likelihood that the project's deliverable remains fit for purpose.
- Suitable user resources can be sourced and committed to the project, increasing the likelihood that its deliverable will be specified and tested according to their preference.
- The project's deliverable will only be released into the post-project environment when the User authority has provided their approval, thereby reducing the likelihood that it will be unsuitable for operational use.

Responsibilities:

- to ensure the user expectations of the project and its intended deliverable are specified;
- to ensure the user community's expectations of a successful outcome are managed;
- to translate user matters and brief relevant stakeholders such that well-informed decisions may be taken;
- to represent user views and opinions and provide authoritative arbitration where necessary;
- to set up and chair a User Forum, if necessary, within which user concerns may be aired and managed;
- to secure and commit user resources to the project;
- to approve the Project Plan from the user's perspective;
- to agree and authorize each stage plan from a user perspective;
- to arbitrate and resolve user priority or resource conflicts;

- to brief and advise user management on all matters that may affect them, where this is beyond the remit of the Project Manager;
- to ensure the impact of potential change is evaluated from a user perspective;
- to ensure that user actions to mitigate risks are discharged in accordance with the Risk Register;
- to assure the project's management team that quality control procedures are being applied such that the user's expectations can be met;
- to recommend project closure once the project's deliverable has met specified user expectations.

Reporting to:

- Sponsor.

Reporting from:

- Project Manager (through Project Steering Group);
- User Forum (where implemented).

Deliverables:

- list of user project success criteria (contained in the Business Case);
- approved Requirements Specification;
- approved User Acceptance Test Plan;
- approved User Acceptance Tested Solution;
- implementation Approval Decision (with Project Steering Group).

Measures of success:

- robustness of definition of user success criteria;
- approval of a solution which meets user success criteria;
- clear and authoritative user contribution to change control process;
- successful arbitration of disputes and conflict within user community;
- clear and authoritative user contribution to testing of solution;
- clear and authoritative user contribution to project closure decision.

Considering the Specialist authority, the role may be defined as follows:

Role purpose:

- To deliver a solution which meets the requirements specified by the users and which conforms to all necessary specialist constraints.

Benefits of role:

- The needs of the specialists are given a profile, increasing the likelihood that the project's deliverable will meet user expectations and conform to all necessary specialist constraints.
- Change Requests can be promoted or challenged by a champion, increasing the likelihood that the project's deliverable remains fit for purpose.
- Suitable specialist resources can be sourced and committed to the project, increasing the likelihood that its deliverable will be developed, tested and delivered according to the design.
- The project's deliverable will only be released into the post-project environment when the Specialist authority has provided their approval, thereby reducing the likelihood that it will be too challenging to maintain.

Responsibilities:

- to ensure the specialist expectations of the project and its intended deliverable are specified;
- to ensure the specialist community's expectations of a successful outcome are managed;
- to ensure the solution meets the user community's requirements;
- to translate specialist matters and brief relevant stakeholders such that well-informed decisions may be taken;

- to represent specialist views and opinions and provide authoritative arbitration where necessary, especially where external suppliers have been engaged;
- to secure and commit specialist resources to the project;
- to approve the Project Plan from the specialist's perspective;
- to agree and authorize each stage plan from a specialist perspective;
- to arbitrate and resolve specialist priority or resource conflicts;
- to brief and advise specialist management on all matters that may affect them, where this is beyond the remit of the Project Manager;
- to ensure the impact of potential change is evaluated from a specialist perspective;
- to ensure that specialist actions to mitigate risks are discharged in accordance with the Risk Register;
- to assure the project's management team that quality control procedures are being applied such that specialist constraints can be met;
- to recommend project closure once the project's deliverable has met specified specialist expectations.

Reporting to:

- Sponsor.

Reporting from:

- Project Manager (through Project Steering Group).

Deliverables:

- managed suppliers (external and internal);
- list of specialist project success criteria (contained in the Business Case);
- approved Solution Design;
- approved specialist deliverables (prior to user acceptance test);
- implementation Approval Decision (with Project Steering Group).

Measures of success:

- robustness of definition of specialist success criteria;
- delivery of a solution which meets user success criteria;
- delivery of a solution which conforms to solution design;
- clear and authoritative specialist contribution to change control process;
- successful arbitration of disputes and conflict within specialist/supplier community;
- clear and authoritative specialist contribution to testing of solution;
- clear and authoritative specialist contribution to project closure decision.

Taking the Case study as an example, a candidate Project Steering Group might have been formed as follows:

FIGURE 3.3

For this group to work effectively, the sponsor would have to be suitably motivated and incentivized to perform the role, in addition to having a proper understanding of the responsibilities.

There might also be a risk that they might confuse the BAU reporting line from the selected regional sales manager with the relationship they have with that same person in their role as User authority on the Project Steering Group. And that same person would have to be sufficiently confident of themselves to stand up to their BAU manager (the sales director) in their role as project sponsor. But assuming that these challenges could be discussed and overcome, the model above might work well for the project in question.

Identify and contain the responsibilities and authority of the Project Manager

The concerns a Project Manager has about their senior team's competence are often matched by the senior team's unrealistic expectations of their Project Manager. It is crucial that the role of Project Manager is as tightly defined and managed as any other so that both parties have a clear and common understanding of the boundary between them. Here is what the Project Steering Group may expect from their Project Manager:

Role purpose:

- To deliver the project's deliverable in accordance with the most recently authorized expectations of timescale, cost and quality.

Benefits of role:

- Increases the likelihood that the project will meet its varied expectations through the provision of a planned, coordinated effort.
- Mitigates the risks of failure due to inadequacy of planning, monitoring or control.
- Allows for the provision of accurate management information, thereby enabling timely and effective corrective action.
- Provides leadership and motivation for the team, thereby maximizing productivity.
- Allows for the use of recognized and proven principles and techniques to be used, thereby reducing the likelihood of rework.

Responsibilities:

- to develop, and seek approval for, a plan to initiate and deliver the project;
- to maintain the Project Plan within identified constraints;
- to manage project changes/risks/issues;

- to identify and delegate work packages to relevant work streams;
- to motivate and coordinate the project team and other personnel involved in the project;
- to monitor, report and control progress against plan, escalating when outside of agreed escalation conditions;
- to maintain effective communications and expectations with stakeholders (internal or external) and propose solutions to resolve conflicts;
- to maintain project metrics, including time, cost, quality and benefits tracking;
- to maintain the Business Case on behalf of the Project Steering Group to allow for their continued assessment of project viability;
- to implement and operate effective change management;
- to develop and present evidence to allow for the managed closure of the project.

Reporting to:

- Project Steering Group.

Reporting from:

- Work Stream Leaders.

Deliverables:

- contributions to maintained Business Case;
- maintained Project Plan;
- maintained Risk Register;
- maintained Change Control Log;
- regular Project Forecast Reports;
- Project Closure Report.

Measures of success:

- the extent to which there is an authorized plan that shows progress to date and forecasts for time, cost and quality;
- the extent to which escalation conditions for time and cost have been agreed with the Project Steering Group and are being applied;

- the extent to which there is a record demonstrating that any changes to scope, timescale, cost and benefits have been approved by those who have authority to do so;
- the extent to which there is a record of risks to the project, together with mitigation plans and actions;
- the extent to which the Project Steering Group is being kept regularly and sufficiently informed through progress/forecast reports;
- the extent to which the most recently authorized expectations of time, cost and quality have been met.

Considering the management hierarchy of Project Manager, Project Steering Group and Change Management Team, the contract between them can be summarized thus:

The CMT identifies, commissions and delivers a value-adding mix of projects within a budget, aligned with the strategic and commercial imperatives set out by the business. It delegates the responsibility for the successful delivery of each project to suitably authoritative Project Steering Groups whose job it is to clearly define and deliver the benefits. They contract with their Project Manager that the manager will develop a plan which shows the extent to which their wishes may be realized, and that on agreement between them all, the Project Manager will deliver the intended product on time and budget.

Define, separate and control the levels of authority

For the hierarchy to work effectively requires that measures and controls are placed around the limits of authority awarded to each body within it. Failing to do so simply encourages the confusion of responsibilities which were prevalent in the Case study. Such control is achieved by defining some escalation conditions. These are criteria which help to ensure that each body – CMT, Project Steering Group, Project Manager and Work Stream Leaders – understands where the boundary lies between their span of authority and that of those above and/or below them. When practised, this is sometimes referred to as 'management by exception'.

It works on the premise that each layer in the management hierarchy has a greater degree of authority than the one beneath it, just like the BAU line structure. Furthermore – and crucially – it assumes that no one in the hierarchy would wish their reports to exceed their limit of authority, as to do so would mean that improperly authorized decisions were being made, thereby undermining the whole structure.

These defined levels of authority become especially relevant when an issue is faced, or a change is requested that may risk the project missing its intended benefits, time or cost targets. So each body in the hierarchy requires a specified measure of authority within which they carry out their responsibilities. Agreeing such measures in advance, and having them form part of the change management culture in an organization, enables all parties to escalate matters under controlled conditions, removing the confusion of who is authorized to take charge when problems or changes arise.

Here is an example illustrating how the approach may be practically implemented. The Project Steering Group provides its Project Manager with a degree of time and budgetary flexibility so that he or she may act on their own authority within pre-agreed constraints. So if the escalation conditions for time and cost have been set for ±two weeks and ±5 per cent respectively, the Project Steering Group need not be involved in or troubled by the daily management of the project as long as its forecast end date does not vary by more or less than two weeks and the forecast cost remains within ±5 per cent of its target. If at any time the Project Manager forecasts that the project will not be completed within the agreed escalation conditions, the problem must be escalated immediately to the Project Steering Group for a decision on how to proceed as the Project Manager's boundaries of authority have been breached. Crucially, escalation conditions do not mean that the Project

Steering Group is allowing their Project Manager to overspend or deliver late. The conditions provide the flexibility which the Project Manager will need to allow their daily management of the project to continue unhindered, whilst underlining the Project Steering Group's power to act if the project should be forecast to veer too far off track.

The Project Manager can be required to implement a similar set of escalation conditions with their direct reports (the Work Stream Leaders) so that any possibility of a late or over-costly delivery is identified, escalated and managed well in advance.

Above the Project Steering Group sits the CMT whose interest in the costs and benefits is their greatest priority. So they may institute a set of escalation conditions with all of their Project Steering Groups, requiring them to provide an alert if the forecast benefits appear at any time to be insufficient to outweigh the eventual expenditure. In this way, the CMT can use its greater authority to manage the possible variance.

A red, amber and green coding system is often used to illustrate the forecast condition of each project. This is sometimes known as 'RAG' reporting. Red denotes a forecast that is outside an escalation condition. Amber means that the project is off target but still within the designated manager's span of authority to control. Green means it remains on target.

Conclusion

This chapter has considered what, in summary, might be described as the redesign and reorganization of those people in an organization who are engaged in the change agenda. There are considerable consequences.

Roles, many of which may be entirely new to the organization, will have to be clearly and commonly understood, so an enterprise-wide training or communications exercise may be necessary. Making it stick will be equally challenging; breaches and misunderstandings must be acted upon if a gradual slipping backwards is to be avoided.

As sponsors and Project Steering Groups assume a greater role in projects, some Project Managers may consider their own authority to have been reduced, and feel emasculated. It will be necessary to deal with this sensitively as such people may well have carried a great burden for the organization. They should not be persecuted for working practices which were not of their own making.

Some people, sponsors included, may simply not come up to the mark. As you compare your organization's preferred and actual competencies, it may become apparent that the corporate change-capability pool is smaller or shallower than you thought. Shortfalls in junior positions are easier to fill with contract resource than senior ones.

The positive benefits clearly outweigh such challenges. The organization will be able to take greater control of its change agenda through a more stable and structured management hierarchy. As the pool of competent change practitioners grows, the success of the business's portfolio of projects will be driven by a broader, richer range of skills, knowledge, experience, character and authority. Better and more timely decisions will be made, increasing the likelihood of delivering what the organization intended.

And the engagement of Project Steering Groups should allow a clearer expression of project success to be defined and communicated, as the following chapter will describe.

SUMMARY

- Separate and clarify the roles which are required within the change management environment.
- Select and engage incumbents who are qualified for the roles.
- Place great emphasis on the suitability of the sponsors (a great project manager is scant compensation for a poor sponsor).
- Empower project participants, but only with defined and contained parameters of authority.
- Educate the workforce to understand the interdependence of the roles.
- Employ Project Steering Groups to encourage balanced decision making within projects.
- It takes an organization to deliver a project – and the organization must itself be organized to do so!

CHAPTER FOUR

ARTICULATE AND COMMUNICATE THE VISION

This chapter covers:

- the importance of a clear vision to provide focus for the organization's energies;
- the ways in which a vision may be articulated;
- the need for the continued engagement of stakeholders throughout;
- the need to employ a form of governance for the initiative which is suited to the vision.

Every one of us has a very particular perspective on the world, born of our experience, concerns, relationships and prejudices. It is no different in and around projects. Anyone given the opportunity to understand a project will create an interpretation of it which suits their specific interests. That interpretation will be unique and different from the views others may have. So it is both wrong and unhelpful when we assume that:

Myth 4: Everyone knows what we want to achieve.

In this chapter, we will discover that one perspective of success often looks very different from another and that it is crucial for organizations to allow the vision for their projects to be defined, developed and revised until everyone shares a clear and common understanding.

CASE STUDY

Where previously the technology underpinning several of an organization's key systems had proven unstable and unreliable, a specialist proposed that a change of database would allow for a greater ease of maintenance, capacity for growth, and reduced risk of system failure. There would be many technical complexities to overcome, but a transformational project was conceived at the heart of the IT division to meet every challenge and deliver the objectives.

As soon as the idea was floated, there was immediate interest across the organization. Given that the systems had been troublesome for so long, nearly everyone could see a means of achieving something beneficial from a project to improve the database. The users of the systems saw beyond a solution to the technical problems that they faced every day and anticipated a suite of fresh functionality to provide new products and services to their customers. On hearing of such potential, the organization's commercial managers began to predict increased revenues and an improved competitive position amongst their rivals. And even within the IT division from where the idea had originated, specialists from far and wide conceived of ways in which they might participate in, contribute to and gain from the project.

The project was given a name and its many followers became early disciples, seeking to promote its worth amongst those who would secure the funding. With so much goodwill behind it and the lure of benefits to so many stakeholders, it took on a priority quite unmatched by anything else the business was seeking to undertake. It was the solution to so many problems and opportunities. Hopes ballooned.

Yet the project ran into difficulties almost immediately. Although great care had been taken to accommodate the many stakeholders into the project, the Project Steering Group (PSG) was so large as to render it almost unable to make any decisions. And since the interests of its members were so diverse and (in many cases) antagonistic, the sponsor had terrific trouble trying to maintain any semblance of order.

This had an effect on the Project Manager who had to interpret the expectations of a PSG above him which could not speak with one voice. Since the PSG members were each pursuing an agenda of their own, they offered little instruction to the Project Manager short of requiring him to meet their particular objectives, and to overcome the persistent stream of problems the project faced daily.

Without a clear expectation of scope or vision, the project progressed through an extraordinary cycle of growth and division, rather like the way in which the cells of an embryo multiply. New sub-projects and work streams were a constant feature as fresh activity was identified or invented. Since clear boundaries had not been set, it was hard to argue for their exclusion. This, of course, had a significant impact on the size of the budget. In the early days, the project was able to justify further claims on the organization's purse by using the argument that any early estimates on a project of this size would be inaccurate. But such reasoning soon wore thin, especially when other more vital, interesting or demanding initiatives or BAU activity sought to compete for funds. And as the budget grew, the argument in favour of its benefits became ever more laboured. The business continued to pump investment into the project, yet the vision, such as it was, seemed never any closer or tangible.

The problems on the project reached a pitch when, one afternoon, the core members of the PSG met informally to consider how to control what had become a leviathan. The IT director, the project's senior-most technology specialist, advanced the view that the vision had changed and grown by such a margin that it was almost impossible to know what the objectives were. Several other directors representing the myriad of departments who would use the new systems nodded in agreement. The sponsor – the business's operation's director – snapped. Under pressure from inside and outside the project, he banged the table with his fist and exclaimed, 'Everyone knows what we want to achieve!' Then he laid out a view of a successful outcome which was so alien or irrelevant or inconsistent with the views of those others around the table that it served only to demonstrate how untrue his statement really was.

The project had become so large, unwieldy and directionless that any solution short of cancellation would be seen as a commitment to further pain and confusion. Coincidentally, and perhaps serendipitously, the sponsor had reached his retirement age and his departure provided an opportunity for a regime change. The organization's chief executive appointed a new sponsor with a very specific brief; a month later, it was announced that the project was to be cancelled.

What this means

A project's stakeholders may be very great in number but of varied importance

Even the smallest of projects can have a significant number of stakeholders, from those who state the need and use the product, to those involved in its design and delivery. The Case study focused on an enormous initiative whose stakeholders included not only a large multiple of internal parties, but also several external technology suppliers. The knee-jerk response was to have a representative of each stakeholder-cluster participate in the Project Steering Group, the premise being that in this way, they would have a role to play. What the sponsor in the Case study failed to account for was that not every stakeholder should have a *management* role. So in a forum where everyone was free to air their views, the voice of management was lost and the vision could not be formed.

Whether or not the project succeeds, the PSG is accountable

As the PSG grew in size, the responsibility for success or failure became ever more thinly spread amongst the members until the burden on each of them was so little that few felt any sense of accountability.

People have different and conflicting views of what success looks like

In the previous chapter, three perspectives were described which it is sensible to embed and protect in any project. They were:

- the commercial perspective, represented in the Project Steering Group as the sponsor;
- the user perspective, represented in the Project Steering Group as the User authority;
- the specialist perspective, represented in the Project Steering Group as the Specialist authority.

Anyone involved in the project, and especially those who participate in the Project Steering Group, will consider success from one of these unique and different perspectives. So the Case study's sponsor wanted to ensure that the revenue-generating opportunities offered by the improved technology were maximized. The users were less interested in the commercial measurement of the project, and more attracted by the prospect of improved systems and functionality. And the specialists sought a solution that would reduce their maintenance workload. As each pursued their separate vision, the project was pulled in at least three separate directions.

Success is achieved at different times for different stakeholders

The sponsor maintained that success would be achieved when the benefits of the database conversion filtered through into an increase in sales revenues. This might take months or years. However, the user and specialist community might both have expected an earlier reward. As soon as the new systems became available (and regardless of whether they generated any new revenues), the IT specialists might have hoped for a swift reduction in the number of faults arising from database failures. And the users would have expected immediate access to the wider range of functions and services offered by the new applications. Yet as things stood, it was all or nothing. Everyone's success depended on the end of the project and since this appeared to be slipping further and further away, so too did the promise of any reward. That the sponsor's return on investment was the furthest target of all simply added to the pressure he and the business were under.

As projects change, they may pursue a new course which threatens divergence from the corporate change agenda

As the project changed in almost every measure, it drifted further away from the original expectation it had promised to meet. Whilst it is not wrong or even unlikely that the shape of a project can change, those changes must be understood and controlled. In this way, management retain their authority over the project, and allow for compensations to be made if the original vision looks likely to be missed. During the Case study, there was virtually no evidence of change control. This is a subject so significant that it will be covered in a chapter of its own.

The project manager is not responsible for defining the vision

As the previous chapter argued, the Project Manager has an important but limited role. In the Case study, a good deal of his time was spent attempting to translate a vision into a plan. Since the vision itself was incoherent, it should not have come as a surprise that the plan followed suit. Yet the fault is not automatically that of the Project Manager; the plan, organization structure and governance derive from understanding the vision. If it is ill formed, so too will be almost every aspect of the project.

The consequences of ignoring the imperative

The challenge of the change will be misunderstood

Misunderstanding the vision may have one of two consequences. Either change initiatives will tinker with, but not transform, the business. As a result, the benefits may fail to be at all remarkable. Or the organization will bite off more than it can chew, and costs will spiral, again with a damaging impact on the benefits.

With a misunderstanding prevalent at senior levels, Project Managers will be poorly directed, or directed to deliver the wrong thing. At best, products will be created but behaviours won't change. Projects will have failed to contribute positively to the forward movement of the organization.

The governance instituted to deliver change will be unsuitable

Suitable change governance derives from a clear and common understanding of the vision it must achieve. If the vision is unclear, the governance which arises to deliver it will be dysfunctional. PSGs will be formed of the wrong participants, will become unable to make authoritative decisions and will lose the respect they deserve and authority they need. Plans will fail to identify and direct the right activities, and controls will fail to work in the absence of any sensible baseline against which to measure variance. Instead of risks, issues will dominate the agenda, diverting energy and any sense of direction the project may have had.

People won't understand or engage in the delivery of change

As evidence mounts that projects are failing to meet their expectations, enthusiasm to participate will lessen. Senior stakeholders will become disillusioned and less ready to engage in future initiatives, project managers and team members will shy away from the apparent chaos, and visionaries – the sources of creativity – will be disinclined to promote their ideas because of the organization's inability to translate them through effective change management into sustainable benefits.

The solutions

Identify the stakeholders

On 25 May 1961, the American president John F Kennedy said: 'I believe that this nation should commit itself to achieving the goal, before this decade is out, of landing a man on the moon and returning him safely to the Earth.' This clear, measurable rallying cry galvanized the energy and enthusiasm of a nation and resulted in the extraordinary spectacle on 20 July 1969 of the first manned mission to land on the moon. If the vision statement had been any more verbose than the president's pithy 31 words, it would have lost its power and impact to motivate. But behind that statement would have been an enormous set of expectations from others which, if the initiative was to maintain momentum and focus for almost a decade, would require analysis, expression, communication and promotion. If a vision is to be shared, it is only to be expected that people will wish to contribute to it.

Any project's vision must accommodate and express the wishes of the three perspectives described earlier: the user, specialist and commercial interests. Yet each will already have their own preferred way of articulating what is important to them. At some point, the users will expect to complete a needs statement. On receipt, the specialists will intend to develop a solution outline. And to justify the entire initiative, the sponsor should seek to construct a commercial cost-justification. What makes a well-articulated vision really effective is when it is able to capture elements of each, and express them together in a clear, complete and coherent manner such that the vision itself, and everything which follows, is *consistent*. When these three expressions come together, the vision can begin to do more than simply list the needs of the various stakeholder groups. The confluence of expectations allows for the true purpose of the initiative to be developed, going so far even as to explain what cultural shifts are necessary if true change is to be realized.

As sponsor, President Kennedy sought for his nation to conquer space and gain political capital and power from so doing. The television-watching public sought pride in its country's achievements and expected to see them played out across the world's media. The scientific community hoped for advances and learning, expecting that experiments would be conducted and materials from the moon returned to Earth. The astronauts would have been comforted by the president's last six words, but may have had expectations of their own. They may have wished to exercise considerable control over the various vehicles in which they were to be transported, that their families would be cared for by the nation in the event of an accident, or simply that they would be able to see outside the spacecraft (early designs famously had no windows).

In drawing together these expressions, a considerably larger but more complete vision emerges, perhaps lacking the impact of the president's précis, but presenting a fuller picture which allows for the removal of inconsistencies, and accommodates the compromises necessary for a tract which eventually speaks for everyone.

In understanding this, a plan may be built which takes account of the vision, and seeks to aid its delivery. So, if the vision required the nation to feel 'pride', the plan would have had to help deliver it by, for example, ensuring that all significant stages of the journey were televised live. And if the scientific community's expectation was for 'technological advance', the plan would have needed to allow for a spacecraft design which could accommodate the return of materials to Earth for analysis. And in so many more ways, the vision would mould the plan.

To return to what is, literally, the *real* world, the project visions of organizations like our own may be as complex yet are too often promoted in too simplistic a form. How does one begin to capture and articulate the vision?

FIGURE 4.1

Figure 4.1 outlines the general areas in which people from each of the three perspectives might be expected to show greatest interest.

The commercial or strategic community

Matters that will be of greatest interest to the sponsor will be those which are most likely to affect the commercial and strategic vision for the project, as it is in these precise areas that they are expected to demonstrate greatest competence and enthusiasm. The expression of a commercial vision in the form of a Business Case or cost-justification will be considered in detail in the next chapter. What are less easy to capture are statements which describe the behavioural and cultural changes expected, and upon which the realization of benefits depend. Some examples are included later in this chapter.

The user community

The user community – and the User authority in particular – are most interested in the fitness for purpose of the deliverables the project creates. They are keen that the *quality* of the project's deliverable is as expected. And if they have trouble expressing what they mean by quality, others will have difficulty developing and delivering it.

'Quality' might be defined as the total set of features and characteristics of a product or service which bear on its ability to satisfy stated needs. So the users may express their vision in terms of the features and characteristics they are expecting from the project's main deliverable, commonly captured in a 'user needs specification'. However, a statement of desired features is hardly a vision and can divert attention from other matters which may be of even greater importance. For instance, the vision for users of a computer system may be to remove their daily dependence on the IT department who perform a range of technical support activities. So in addition to the more usual expectation of certain functional requirements is the aspiration for 'user independence', a vision which is harder to define but which is no less relevant to the users than the features they expect to be delivered.

Figure 4.1 lists just some of the additional features and characteristics that may matter to the community of people who will use the project's output. It is by no means complete, but it does perhaps demonstrate that delivering them a product is only a part of what they have in mind.

The specialist community

Initially, the vision of the specialists may be to deliver a solution which meets the needs of the users and does so within the prevailing policies and regulations. But when one probes further into the specialists' expectations, fitness for purpose and compliance may be but their outward projection. Additional and hidden aspirations for the project may also include a wish to build something which is ground-breaking, creative or innovative – something which will cause others to reflect on its elegance or beauty.

Articulate the vision

As the *true* vision is revealed, it becomes easier to conceive of a plan to meet it, or to seek compromises which rein in the expectations of stakeholders. But gaining insight into the various stakeholders' expectations is an entire challenge of its own.

Ask the stakeholders what they are expecting

Having instituted a Project Steering Group (or having at least identified the project's commercial, user and specialist authorities), convene a meeting of the Project Steering Group. In preparation, ask each member: *'How would you describe your vision for the project?'* Participants should describe their vision as a series of bulleted statements (see later examples), not as a series of wordy paragraphs from which the vision must be teased.

The sponsor must be especially well briefed since they have an additional responsibility to manage disagreements and confusion. When the group is together, seek to gain mutual understanding of each person's perspectives. They may be steered by reference to some of the typical differences between their various perspectives (as identified in Figure 4.1), and provided with a range of examples (see later in this chapter). Of particular importance is to have them express their expectations fully. The SMART approach is always helpful: you are looking for statements which are Specific, Measurable, Achievable, Realistic and Timely. Check each one against these characteristics. Then, take each of the three perspectives (commercial, user and specialist) in turn and have them further develop and refine a list to which they can commit.

Ask the stakeholders what matters most

When the various statements have been pulled together into a single list, one further question is necessary to *really* test understanding and commitment: *'In what order should these vision statements be prioritized?'* At the very least, the aim should be to develop a list in which the criteria have been ranked in order of high, medium and low priority. In this way, it is possible to determine not only what matters most, but also in what order parts of the project might be cut back should there be a need to change the plan later on. It is really far better to have these discussions in the formative stages of the project rather than when it is well underway since it helps to articulate the vision, provide focus to the plan and serve as a basis against which change-control decisions may be more readily made.

Identify contradictions and broker compromises

Consider the Case study: the User authority has a vision in which two new product sets may be launched for the customer. However, the IT specialists insist that the existing database servers can presently accommodate the addition of only one. The users argue that they are falling behind their competitors and that any delay in the introduction of a second product set will weaken their position in the market. The IT specialists maintain that the entire business will be placed at risk if the database is put under any greater pressure. A conclusion to the mismatched expectations is needed, especially so that the Project Manager may be provided with a clear set of priorities on which to base the plan. So the sponsor arbitrates and compromises are sought. It is proposed that after the first product set has been launched, the database servers are replaced. Then all existing products will be made available to customers via the web. Thereafter, the database software itself will be replaced, followed by the introduction of the second product set.

In this way, the vision becomes a more realistic and consistent expression of compromises, yet one which unifies the various stakeholders.

Capture and secure the vision

Whilst many things around us may change, the fundamental vision for a project should remain relatively stable throughout its lifetime. Even if something happens to cause a substantial rethink, it is important to have an articulated expectation against which to determine the impact of a change.

The route to obtain a consistent, prioritized, non-contradictory and SMART vision may not be an easy one. The risks of failing include the following:

- If the vision is unclear, the project may be unsuccessful in meeting expectations, resulting in a delay to implement the solution or, at worst, a failure to achieve the expected benefits.
- If the commercial vision is unclear, money may be invested in an initiative which might have been better spent elsewhere.
- If the vision is not articulated to a low enough level of detail, it may be misinterpreted, thereby causing a failure to achieve success.
- If priorities are unclear, changes will be considerably harder to manage, resulting in time delays and budgetary challenges.
- If the vision is unclear, it will be more difficult to motivate and direct the team, resulting in the expense of confusion and rework.

The bulleted, prioritized list of expectations which has been created by this process becomes the vision. A summary paragraph may be developed to sell the project – JFK had his 31 words – but for a robust expression on the back of which a plan may be created, substance is essential. Whilst many people have trouble understanding why a project generates so much documentation, there are some absolutely essential written reports which capture the answers to the project's most important questions. The Business Case is one of these and is often considered a suitable repository for the vision. The next chapter considers this important topic.

An example of a vision

A company regularly facilitates the delivery of public conferences through the year. Paying delegates are invited to hear speakers talk on a range of topics. For one specific conference, the project organization is as follows:

FIGURE 4.2

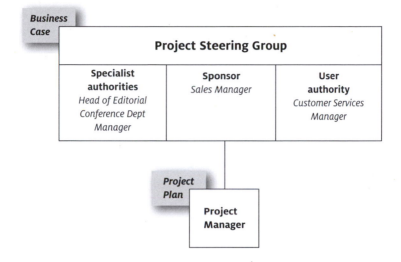

Simply put, the vision for the project may be described thus:

- to deliver a conference on a topic of relevance to delegates and which is attractive enough to a sufficient number of them that a profit is made, and that this event enables us to leverage more business in the future.

Yet if each participant from the Project Steering Group were to be interrogated further, it is likely that a greater and more revealing level of detail could be discovered. For example:

Commercial authority (Sales Manager):

- the sum of delegate revenues outweighs the total costs of running the conference (by a specific margin);
- the specified budget is not exceeded unless there are revenues which compensate;
- all delegate revenues are received before the event takes place (ie there are no 'bad debts' or delegates at the conference who have not paid in full in advance);
- no fewer than 3 per cent of delegates book on another conference within a year.

Given the second half of the vision statement, the project sponsor is seeing this conference not only as an immediate profit-generating exercise, but as an opportunity to build future business. This aspiration is translated into a meaningful target (the last criterion) which must be met if the vision is to be fully realized. The project will complete just after the conference itself has ended. However, it will not be possible to determine whether this final measure of success has been achieved until a year has passed. This carries two consequences:

- The 'Benefits Realization' period after the project will last a year, during which the sponsor should retain an interest and ensure that *actual* benefits are measured.
- The Project Manager should ensure that suitable delegate records are taken which allow for the measurement of repeat bookings to take place.

It is only in this way that it will ever be possible to know whether the vision has been achieved.

Specialist authority (Head of Editorial):

- The factual content of the conference material is accurate.
- Conference content is up to date.
- The agenda content is not influenced by the commercial interests of the sponsor.

Specialist authority (Conference Department Manager):

- The conference agenda is organized logically.
- There are frequent breaks.
- The most engaging speaker is placed in the agenda slot after lunch.
- Each conference speaker has an understudy.
- All speakers will have performed well at a previous conference conducted by ourselves.
- Confirmation of attendance will have been received from each speaker no later than two months before the conference, and no later than two weeks before the publication of the conference marketing materials.

Notice how the Head of Editorial Specialist authority has made it abundantly clear that they expect to maintain absolute editorial independence from the Sales Manager. This may cause conflict between the two parties, but it is better that any disagreements are managed within the jurisdiction of the project, not least so that the Project Manager can look to a single source (the Project Steering Group) for resolution.

User authority (Customer Services Manager):

- Conference content is as advertised in the marketing materials.
- At least 90 per cent of Conference Appraisal Forms are completed before delegates leave the venue.
- At least 40 per cent of those who complete their Conference Appraisal Forms agree that they would recommend the organization's conferences to a colleague.
- There are no more than two category 1 complaints arising within a week of the completion of the conference.
- Delegates are provided with an opportunity to network with people they have not previously met.
- Delegates have come from industry and social sectors the organization is seeking to attract.
- At least 60 per cent of delegates mark the quality of the venue and associated facilities as 'above average'.
- At least 70 per cent of delegates agree that they have left the conference knowing more than when they arrived.
- At least 85 per cent of delegates consider the conference subject matter to have been relevant.
- At least 75 per cent of delegates consider the speakers to have been engaging and authoritative.

The Customer Services Manager is naturally inclined to consider the project from the perspective of the delegates – that is, both their day job and their focus within the project. The User authority is therefore acting as an advocate for the end customer and the criteria listed above are a detailed interpretation of the delegates' vision to attend a conference which is 'attractive'.

Promote and share the vision

It is vital that the vision carries the authority of those who own it. It is the job of the Project Steering Group (or at least a set of authorities who see the world from the three perspectives described) to define the vision, share and validate it with the Change Management Team.

It must be remembered that the PSG is a body of people, not a meeting. If this senior management team is allowed to grow too large, or comes to see itself as anything less than a group of senior authorities with a shared expectation, it will fail, and so will the project.

However, in some cases, such as that referred to in the Case study, the sheer number of stakeholders who wish to share their opinions and perspectives is so great that gaining their engagement in the vision can seem almost impossible. So although the PSG is charged with responsibility for delivering the vision, the wider organization must be brought along with them from the outset, increasing the likelihood that the eventual changes will become embedded in the organization's psyche. A way in which this early engagement may be practically achieved is through the use of a User Forum, shown in Figure 4.3.

Faced with an enormous variety of departments who wish their interests to be represented – and whom the project is seeking to engage – the User authority creates and chairs a forum. This is the environment within which the expectations of many can be understood and managed. It operates by means of a series of regular, managed meetings which allow the essential two-way communication to be conducted between the project's senior user authority and the wider population. Whilst it may be created to generate an investment of ideas, its greater value is as a means of sharing and gaining commitment to the vision. It is, after all, the body of people who attend who will be expected to adopt the project's outcome and, potentially, change their behaviours.

FIGURE 4.3

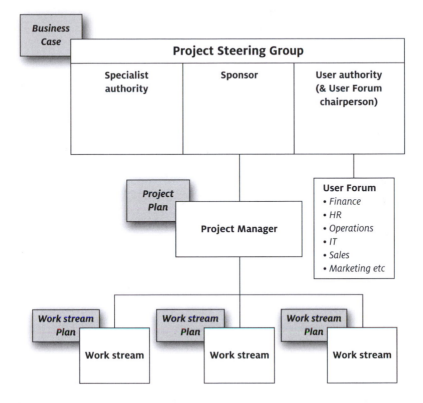

Thereafter, there may be other, complementary communication routes through which to continually remind others of the vision:

- seminars;
- bulletins;
- exhibitions;
- videos;
- web;
- briefings;
- training;
- FAQs;
- face to face;
- intermediaries.

It is also worth acknowledging that not only do we wrongly assume that everyone knows what we want to achieve, but we also wrongly believe that they want to achieve what we want to achieve. There is a variety of ways in which people may be influenced to engage in the journey towards the vision. In the *Journal of Applied Psychology* (August 1980), authors Kipnis, Schmidt and Wilkinson argued in their publication, 'Intraorganization influence tactics: explorations in getting one's way', that when seeking to persuade others of the need to pursue a course, there are seven techniques which can be used in different circumstances:

- consultation – gaining the participation of others in decisions and changes;
- rational persuasion – convincing others by reason or logic;
- inspirational appeals – building enthusiasm by appealing to others' emotions, ideals or values;
- ingratiating tactics – getting someone in a good mood prior to making a request;
- pressure tactics – soliciting compliance or using intimidation and threats;
- upwards appeal – persuading someone on the basis of express or implied support from superiors;
- exchange tactics – making express or implied promises and trading favours;
- coalition tactics – gaining support of others in your effort to persuade someone.

Derive the change initiative's governance from a clear understanding of the vision

Not all change initiatives are projects. There is such a thing as a programme, and contrary to what some might think, it is not simply defined as 'a big project'.

A programme is a vehicle for progressing, coordinating and implementing an organization's strategy, specifically by linking an often complex combination of business-as-usual activity and new projects all focused on the delivery of a defined objective.

The differences between a project and programme can be considered as follows:

FIGURE 4.4

A project...	A programme...
• has relatively few stakeholders;	• has many stakeholders;
• will be a contained disaster if it fails;	• may be a corporate disaster if it fails;
• is focused on a deliverable;	• is focused on a business objective;
• will deliver benefit after completion;	• will deliver benefit in phases;
• has a short- to medium-term lifespan;	• has a long-term lifespan;
• has variable risk;	• is always high risk;
• has a focused scope;	• has a wide scope;
• excludes business-as-usual activity.	• includes business-as-usual activity.

Had the enormity of expectation, risk and consequence been properly understood, the Case study project might have been better recognized – and managed – as a programme. Had the enterprise been seen for what it was, an entirely different way of achieving the vision might have been considered.

Figure 4.5 shows how the initiative was appraised as a project. Since it had first been proposed by the IT division, the approach derived from a technical vision: a new database. A sequential set of activities was conceived to first rebuild the database, then refine or replace the applications which employed it, and finally to adapt the organization's working practices accordingly. But given proper analysis, fixing the database was merely an enabler of greater things. If *those* things had been more clearly identified, the initiative might have been cut in an entirely different way.

FIGURE 4.5

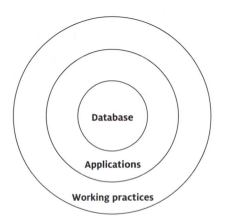

Database

Applications

Working practices

FIGURE 4.6

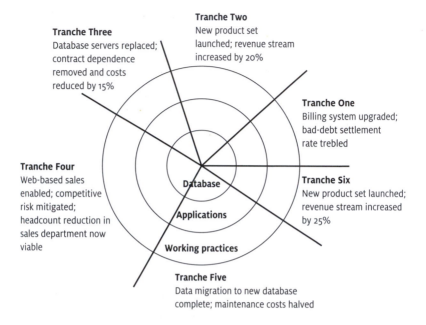

Tranche Two
New product set launched; revenue stream increased by 20%

Tranche Three
Database servers replaced; contract dependence removed and costs reduced by 15%

Tranche One
Billing system upgraded; bad-debt settlement rate trebled

Tranche Four
Web-based sales enabled; competitive risk mitigated; headcount reduction in sales department now viable

Database

Applications

Working practices

Tranche Six
New product set launched; revenue stream increased by 25%

Tranche Five
Data migration to new database complete; maintenance costs halved

The 'tranches' identified in Figure 4.6 might be projects within the wider programme, or a combination of projects and BAU activity. But in either case, each tranche is focused on delivering a set of benefits which outweigh the investment made thus far. So each tranche moves the business closer to the vision whilst delivering injections of benefit along the way, as illustrated in Figure 4.7.

This approach might have been unpalatable to the IT specialists, who might complain at the inelegance of fixing the database in stages, but it would have ensured that the vision remained achievable, progressively delivering some much-needed return on investment, and removing the 'all-or-nothing' risk which hung over, and eventually killed, the project.

FIGURE 4.7

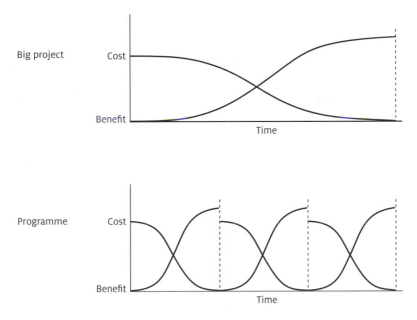

Big project

Programme

Conclusion

Not only is it crucial to have the vision capture the wide range of expectations held by the stakeholders of the change, it is also vital for it to be presented in a form which suits the audience. In attempting to pull together and balance people's varied aspirations, you'll probably spend longer trying to define what you thought was a simple premise, but gain a clearer and more intimate understanding of the true objective. By sharing the vision with others, you'll run up against conflicts and challenges, but in dealing with them earlier will be more able to achieve compromise and engagement. And having stress tested things in this way, the governance you put in place to manage change will be more suited to the vision you are seeking to deliver, and the plans will be better aligned to it.

SUMMARY

- A vision must be more than a rallying cry if it is to serve as a statement of direction and as a basis for the plan.
- A vision must do more than express the expectations of a limited population.
- For others to engage, it is advantageous that they see some benefit for themselves in the vision.
- When suitably structured, a Project Steering Group can serve as the authority who direct others towards the vision.
- A project is not the only management vehicle by which to deliver change – a programme allows for incremental, value-adding steps towards the vision.

CHAPTER FIVE

JUSTIFY EVERY INVESTMENT

This chapter covers:

- the unique and crucial role played by the Business Case;
- the importance of commercially quantifying the intended benefits;
- the value of a disciplined initiation process;
- the opportunity offered by the post-project 'Benefits Realization' period.

The previous chapter considered the importance of a clear and unifying vision for a project. Sometimes, a simply stated vision can suggest benefits so compelling that we might wonder what prevents us from pursuing them. If businesses depend on speed, agility and innovation to overcome competitive pressures, anyone promoting caution can be seen as a hindrance. So when a collective euphoria is allowed to outweigh calls of care, an organization can easily – and wrongly – persuade itself that:

Myth 5: Great ideas need no justification.

In this chapter, the huge value and importance of a commercially justifiable argument will be considered, and the case made that an organization should not embark upon any project without one.

CASE STUDY

A not-for-profit organization depended on the contributions of its individual members. In return for their annual fee, members benefited from the range of offers and services the organization provided, including discounts, access to specialist services, political lobbying, publications and the benefit of a unifying 'voice'. A significant proportion of the membership was considered very active, exchanging their ideas, best practices and knowledge, but the means by which they were able to do so were limited. Although there was an incredibly well attended annual conference, it was a rare, expensive and haphazard way for members to network. Furthermore, as the institution had itself grown through the gradual unification of several smaller organizations, it emerged that there were five separate databases and websites, each of which sought to offer support and functionality, but none of which served the whole membership with everything they required. So from the membership's perspective, unification had been achieved, but not integration.

An incoming chairperson decided to address the challenge. Like all previous chairs, she had a two-year tenure and was keen to ensure that a solution was implemented during her period of office. At her inaugural address to the conference, she committed the organization to develop and implement a single membership website which would provide the full range of the services and functions due to all members, and which would enable them to network effectively. It was a statement which won her immediate approval.

The announcement was also well received at the organization's head office. The workforce was burdened by the need to manage data across multiple sites and platforms. The proposed rationalization of systems and databases would mean there was relief in sight.

A project was initiated to deliver the solution. A Project Manager was engaged who, on seeking to develop and gain approval for a Business

Case, was informed that the now mandatory project was a 'no brainer'. Since it was supported by everyone, there was no need for any further justification and he should progress to the planning stage and beyond.

Almost without pausing for breath, a software vendor was commissioned to commence the work, and other projects were either cancelled or put on hold in order to marshal the necessary internal and financial resources.

However, the challenges of the project soon became clearer. The five original websites, although separate, each provided the same essential services but in very different ways. The users of those original websites had become so familiar with them that many were reluctant to see the solution offered in a new way, especially if it meant the adoption of an approach based on one of the other websites. So the process of gathering requirements was not only difficult, but also time consuming and politically charged.

This was exacerbated by expectations from head office staff that new functionality be provided. Since it was they who would be charged with maintaining much of the website's data, they considered their requests to be reasonable, but it merely added a dimension to a project which the chairperson had imagined would be focused only on the membership.

And there were several commercial obstacles. It had been hoped that as the new site went live, it would be possible to decommission the old systems and platforms. However, one of the original websites was maintained under a licence, the contract for which had been renewed only a month prior to the new chairperson's arrival. Although it would be technically possible to remove the website from view, the organization would have to continue paying for it for another two years.

A full year later, debate was still raging about the requirements. The vendor had provided one technical solution after another, each of which was subjected to a further round of discussion and rejection. Of greater concern was the opportunity being lost of implementation before the end of the chairperson's two-year tenure, a political imperative which was of enormous priority, not least to the chairperson. And with this encroaching deadline, the language changed to reflect the pressure; this was now a project which had to be completed before the next conference *at any cost*. But it was only when the accrued costs to date were assessed fully that the truth became clear. In deference to the opinion that the project was incontestable, the vendor's invoices had been paid without question. The dire financial consequences were suddenly realized. Since a budget for the project had never been adequately set, it was difficult to say that it had been exceeded, but it was clear to everyone involved that the project had already sapped much of the organization's available resources, and delivered nothing to date. Not only this, but other projects which might have delivered some value had been postponed or cancelled in favour of the popular favourite. Without any suitable understanding of where the commercial benefits of the project were to come from, it was almost impossible to strip away the least rewarding parts of the potential solution to reveal what might remain of a viable core.

Two years after the chairperson had made her announcement to initiate the project, she stood before the conference and explained how the scope and scale had taken everyone by surprise. Conscious that a key component of her manifesto lay unsatisfied, she nevertheless sought a positive spin, explaining that the new website would complete soon. And, making a commitment which neither she nor her successor could guarantee, added, 'I promise you.'

What this means

A vision must be balanced

As previous chapters have emphasized, the vision must articulate the expectations of the project's user, specialist and commercial interests. The Case study was fundamentally flawed from the moment it decided to forego any commercial verification. Without this, it was unable to take account of critical commercial matters such as the commitment which had been made to a two-year licence for a website which was about to be decommissioned. Instead, the project played to one audience – the users – and spent a large sum of money deliberating what functionality it might deliver them, before considering when or how it might do so.

There is little point in managing the benefits without managing the costs

When asked if they would like a solution which overcomes the challenges they face, no user will decline, not least because it is not they who have to pay. The purpose of the Business Case is not to justify the idea, but the amount one is prepared to spend on its pursuance. In any business, it should not be possible to hold a discussion about the benefits of a project without considering the cost of delivering them. A well-structured Business Case presents an opportunity to compare the benefits with the costs so that a balanced decision may be made. In the Case study, the organization lacked a conscience to temper its enthusiasm; only one side of the argument was heard.

Benefits must be commercially quantified

There are many people who are able to make a compelling argument in favour of their interests. Oratory, eloquence and passion may go a long way in summoning the commitment of others, but there is soon a point at which someone somewhere has to hand over some money. Without knowledge of what one might receive in return for an outlay, an investment is mere spend. So, in committing money to projects, organizations must realize that they are investing in themselves, and that to do so responsibly requires they consider what will be the return on that investment.

In the Case study, the benefits were described in very loose terms: improved networking amongst members, more widely available website functionality, a single front-end portal, former websites decommissioned. Since barely one of these was considered from a commercial perspective, it would have been almost impossible to know when or whether the project could have become a commercial success. Of course, there is a commonly used argument that not all benefits can be commercially quantified and that it is sometimes necessary to commission a project on the basis of its potential unquantified benefits. But let me ask this: if someone was seeking to invest their own money into an enterprise, would they be comfortable that there was only the potential for the return of unquantified benefits? Probably not, so why should we expect anyone with an interest or stake in a formal institution to be any different?

The priority of problems and opportunities will change

The Case study project sought to resolve a problem which had existed for some time, and which, at the point of the new chairperson's accession was of great importance. To begin with, the membership was being offered the promise of a greater networking capability, but as the clock ticked, the imperative became one of delivering before the chairperson's tenure completed. So two years later, the organization faced a new profile of problems (not least the fact that much of its available resource had been misspent!). Projects will do well to capture the imagination and enthusiasm of an organization for much more than a year, no matter how critical they may seem. As interest wanes, so too will the availability of resource. It is vital that there is a substantial and repeatable message which can be enlisted to remind all stakeholders of the relative value of the project. And should it be that there is a greater problem or opportunity to be faced elsewhere, one investment justification can be played off against another.

To facilitate the process of initiation

It is easy to belittle the importance of 'process'. Many organizations will complain that it stifles innovation, dampens enthusiasm and slows responsiveness. Yet the Case study illustrates that, had a little more time been devoted to the justification of the project, it may have been easier to hold it to account. As it was, no budget was set, establishing a commercial culture which was both lax and risky. Nor was a management coalition created to check and balance the aspirations of the chairperson. Every energy was devoted to the undertaking of the project, with precious little focus on challenging its scope, benefits and approach. Initiation, although frustrating for those who wish to promote the project, is at the same time a chance to confirm it as the best way to address a problem, exploit an opportunity or consider an alternative. When that precious window has closed, the costs of reconsidering later will skyrocket.

The consequences of ignoring the imperative

The justification of a project will give a sense of the value it may deliver, so failing to prove a project's commercial viability at the outset means that it becomes more difficult to promote or measure the extent to which any benefits have been delivered at the end. This inability to properly understand value lies at the heart of the risk.

It will follow that a culture which places little emphasis on the management of benefits will probably lose track of what it is spending. At best, it may know the costs but have little idea whether the outcome represents good value.

The consequences go beyond the scope of any single project. The absence of proof will make it harder to obtain investment next time round, especially if funds are being sought from an external investor. And strangely, despite pursuing projects which the organization considers to be 'no brainers', a culture will be created in which ideas are unchallenged and, therefore, where innovation is actually stifled.

Ultimately, the institution will lose control of which projects it undertakes since choice will come down to the eloquence of an argument, or the seniority of the spokesperson. The portfolio of projects will take the organization further and further away from where it really wishes to be. Decision makers will flit from one critical priority to another, with little to discriminate the projects' merits or the arguments used to advocate them.

The solutions

In any walk of life, it is possible to cut corners. To do so may lead to an eventual improvement in a process, or it may increase the risk.

Where change management is concerned, the initiation of a project is often an area where certain stakeholders are keen to remove some of what they consider to be unnecessary or unhelpful bureaucracy. However, what takes place in the early stages of a project's life is critical to its eventual health and that of the organization which sponsors it. If robust, viable, benefit-delivering projects are sought, they must first be identified and defined. The Business Case is central to this process; if it becomes a corner which is cut, the value and purpose of the project may be never properly understood, endorsed or realized.

Use a Business Case to describe, promote and challenge the initiative

A Business Case is a document which serves as a repository for the answers to some of the most crucial questions about the project:

- What is the problem or opportunity?
- What options exist to address it?
- How much must be invested?
- What benefits will it deliver?
- By how much will the benefits outweigh the investment?
- Will the margin be sufficient to justify the investment?
- How will the risks to the venture be mitigated?

The sponsor, as the central commercial authority in the project, must be intimately associated with the Business Case. Even though the Project Manager may have helped to compile it, the sponsor's name should appear clearly on the title page since it is their expression of what a successful outcome will look like.

The intended content is straightforward although the population of the document may be challenging. Here is what one should expect to see in a Business Case (a template is available on the Kogan Page website):

Opportunity or problem: *What is the challenge the project is seeking to address?*

Strategic fit: *Which imperatives does this project seek to advance?*

Interdependencies: *What connections exist between this project and others in the portfolio?*

Success criteria: *What will a successful outcome look like from each of the three perspectives?*

Commercial measures of success.

User measures of success.

Specialist measures of success.

Options considered:

- *Are there a number of alternative ways in which the problem or opportunity may be addressed?*
- *What are the merits or risks of doing nothing?*

Rejected option(s).

Selected option.

Risks.

Benefits.

Costs.

Cost–benefit analysis.

Deliverables and timescales.

Planning assumptions.

Benefits Realization plan: *How will the benefits be measured, implemented and embedded?*

Quantify the benefits you intend to deliver

Since the Business Case is, above all else, an expression of commercial viability, it follows that any proposed benefits must be financially measurable. If they are not, any comparison to the proposed investment will be tenuous at best and those who are asked to commit the money will be unable to make a measured decision. Figure 5.1 highlights the value of comparing like with like.

FIGURE 5.1

Investment	Benefits
Human Resources	Contribution to strategic objectives
Consumables	Efficiency improvements
Marketing materials	New customers
Training	New markets
Services	Protection of income streams
Hardware	Reduction/removal of competitive pressure
Software	Improved customer satisfaction
Environmental	Better colleague motivation
Accommodation	Regulatory compliance
Travel/subsistence	
Severance charges	*Measured in:*
	• *value of increase in revenues*
	• *reduction in overhead costs*
	• *value of increased productivity*
	• *value of mitigated risk*
	Benefits ($)

Most managers would be concerned at the prospect of 'unquantifiable costs', so why are so many people so accepting of 'unquantifiable benefits'? The fact that it can be difficult to quantify benefits does not mean that it should not be done – in fact, it emphasizes the importance even further! So the column on the left identifies the forecast costs, and the sum of these is to be compared with another financial figure – the forecast benefits – at the foot of the right-hand column.

The benefits contained by the bracket are those which are so often included in a Business Case, but too rarely translated into one of the four commercially measurable terms at the bottom. Unless the benefits can be characterized in one of these ways, they should not be taken seriously. For example, if one thrust of an argument in favour of the project is that it will improve customer satisfaction, the challenge must be to translate improved customer satisfaction into a commercially beneficial outcome, such as an increase in revenues arising from a greater number of purchases. So, the Business Case may propose that 'a 5 per cent improvement in customer satisfaction between year 0 and year 1 is envisaged as a direct result of this project. In year 2, it will increase by a further 5 per cent and remain stable during years 3 and 4.' But this alone is insufficient as an argument in favour of funding because there has been no translation of these forecasts into a meaningful, commercial expression. So, the argument must be advanced. More satisfied customers will spend extra on the organization's products and services: a 5 per cent improvement will lead to an increase in sales of $5,000 in year 1 and a further $5,000 in year 2, after which sales will stay at the level of this extra $10,000. The customer satisfaction figures can be measured before and after the project to determine whether the forecast is or was well judged. And if the forecast does not stand up to challenge and scrutiny, why should an investor be expected to put up the funds?

There is a category of project which is regularly and wrongly funded without the challenge of a Business Case: those which are considered mandatory or regulatory. The argument goes that the organization has no choice but to pursue them. This is flawed from the outset since even the most regulated industries can delay, postpone or constrain the scope of projects on which their regulators insist. And, as demonstrated by the Case study, sooner or later the organization will find itself asking how much it is prepared to spend on a project it may not otherwise have chosen to undertake. If only to comprehend and contain the costs of such projects, a Business Case is essential. Since regulatory projects may not deliver an increase in revenues or productivity, nor reduce costs, their benefit will be to ensure the organization mitigates the risks associated with non-compliance, the financial fines and sanctions for which become the project's commercial benefits. In short, such projects are justified on the basis that to do nothing would result in realized risk on which a commercial value may be placed.

Evaluate the margin between the forecast investment and benefits

The point at which an investment is outweighed by the benefits will be some way in the future. How *far* is a question which can be determined by a cost–benefit analysis.

FIGURE 5.2

Year	0	1	2	3	4
Benefits	0	13,000	70,000	71,000	81,000
Costs	2,500	15,850	64,620	27,400	24,250
Net	−2,500	−2,850	5,380	43,600	56,750
Cumulative	−2,500	−5,350	30	43,630	100,380

This simple example compares the investment and the intended returns of a project over time. It shows a healthy return being made on the investment. In year 2 the benefits outweigh the investment and payback is achieved. In years 3 and 4 the margin is forecast to grow substantially. But since all forecasts are no more than estimates, can the prediction be made more realistic and reliable?

The figures used in Figure 5.2 are straightforward and take no account of the value of money over time. Money received in the future is worth less than money received today, which can be invested. Assuming an interest rate of 6 per cent, $1 today will be worth $1.06 in a year's time. To put it another way, getting $1 in a year's time is like getting $0.94 today. So the value of the future return on a project must be discounted in the cost–benefit analysis. This approach to forecasting more realistic monetary values is called discounted cash flow.

Figure 5.3 adds more detail, so the discounted cash flow can be calculated.

FIGURE 5.3

Year	0	1	2	3	4
Benefits	0	13,000	70,000	71,000	81,000
Costs	2,500	15,850	64,620	27,400	24,250
Net	**−2,500**	**−2,850**	**5,380**	**43,600**	**56,750**
Cumulative	**−2,500**	**−5,350**	**30**	**43,630**	**100,380**
Discount factor	1.0	0.94	0.89	0.84	0.79
Discount net	−2,500	−2,689	4,788	36,607	44, 951
Net present value	**−2,500**	**−5,189**	**−401**	**36,207**	**81,158**

Note: figures have been rounded

The first four rows are identical to those used in the straight-forward calculation in Figure 5.2. The new rows allow the net figure to be discounted by a number of percentage points. The discount factor is the amount by which the net figure must be multiplied in order to discount it by a specified amount. It is calculated like this:

$$\frac{1}{(1+i)^n}$$

where 'i' is the rate and 'n' is the number of years hence. So assuming a rate of 6 per cent and a forecast needed for year 2, the calculation would be:

$$\frac{1}{(1+0.06)^2} + \frac{1}{(1.06)^2} - \frac{1}{1.1236} = 0.89$$

The net figure is multiplied by the discount factor to determine a more realistic value, called the net present value, which, when accumulated over time, gives the discounted cash flow. Thus, this project will yield a net present value of $81,158 in year 4. However, compared with the calculation shown in Figure 5.2, the point at which payback is achieved has been pushed one year further into the future, making it less attractive than it appeared in the non-discounted figures.

Compare projects to inform prioritization

Previous chapters have considered the merits of one project compared to another such that priorities may be determined. The internal rate of return (IRR) is a further technique used to facilitate such a comparison. Calculating it is similar to working out the discounted cash flow, but in reverse. In the example illustrated in Figure 5.3, if all the money invested in this project had been borrowed and it broke even, the interest rate paid on that borrowed money would be the IRR. For example, the project yields $36,207 based on a rate of 6 per cent, whereas an interest rate of 200 per cent would give a yield of −$1,237. Somewhere in between is a rate that would give a zero net present value, in this case, roughly 150 per cent. This is the IRR. As a rule of thumb, the higher the IRR the better. However, it fails to take into account the size of the project, so one with a relatively low investment may have the same IRR as one worth many times more.

Initiate projects to facilitate effective and efficient decision making

Whether an organization routinely runs a portfolio of projects or only occasionally sponsors single projects at a time, the challenge that a Business Case encourages is healthy. So the effective initiation of a project can succeed in doing two things:

- confirming the innate viability of the project itself;
- allowing for the comparison of the project with any others in the portfolio (or which are awaiting approval).

Figure 5.4 illustrates the life of the wider change which the project seeks to facilitate. Prior to the project achieving approval and its consumption of a substantial proportion of its resources, there exists a period where the problem or opportunity is examined. A Project Outline can help to articulate the challenge and the rewards sufficiently that the Change Management Team (CMT) is confident enough to invest in the initiation of a project. In considering the Project Outline, the CMT is presented with an opportunity to

FIGURE 5.4

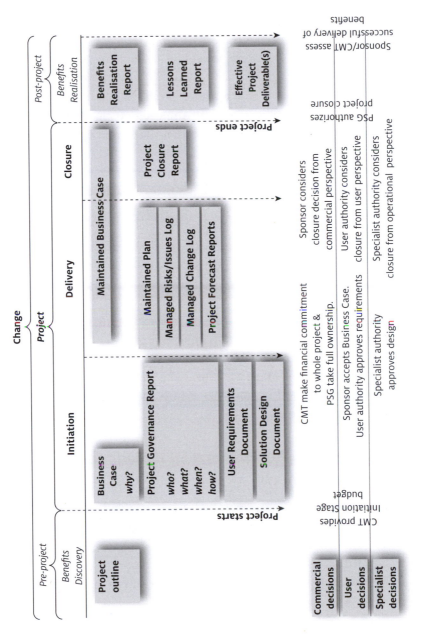

Change

Pre-project		Project				Post-project

Benefits Discovery	Initiation	Delivery	Closure	Benefits Realisation

Project outline

Project starts

Business Case
why?

Project Governance Report
who?
what?
when?
how?

User Requirements Document

Solution Design Document

Maintained Business Case

Maintained Plan

Managed Risks/Issues Log

Managed Change Log

Project Forecast Reports

Project Closure Report

Project ends

Benefits Realisation Report

Lessons Learned Report

Effective Project Deliverable(s)

CMT provides Initiation Stage budget

CMT make financial commitment to whole project & PSG take full ownership.

Sponsor accepts Business Case.
User authority approves requirements

Specialist authority approves design

Sponsor considers closure decision from commercial perspective

User authority considers closure from user perspective

Specialist authority considers closure from operational perspective

PSG authorizes project closure

Sponsor/CMT assess successful delivery of benefits

| **Commercial decisions** |
| **User decisions** |
| **Specialist decisions** |

compare it with any other proposed or actual projects such that their relative priorities may be rechecked. Should they decide to make a commitment to the proposed project, the CMT would usually invest only enough to see the project to a point at which a more fully informed decision may be made as to its prospects. Thus, the approval of the Project Outline should signify the commencement of the development of a Business Case which seeks to explain more fully *why* the project is necessary. Alongside, as the sponsor creates a more complete justification, it is not uncommon for a Project Manager to commence the development of a Project Governance Report (PGR) (a template for which is also included on the Kogan Page website). This document seeks to answer the four remaining, crucial questions about the proposed project:

- Who will be the stakeholders and what responsibilities will they be asked to discharge?
- What must the project deliver?
- When must it achieve its key milestones?
- How much will the project cost to deliver?

When considered together, the Business Case and PGR provide the CMT with much of what they need to make an informed investment decision, not only taking account of the specific merits and risks of the project in question, but also seeing it within the context of the entire change agenda.

Understand the commercial dependence between projects

Projects in a programme may sometimes be considered differently. Individual projects are not necessarily expected to generate a straightforward commercial benefit. What they must do is show how they will use their funding efficiently in order that the benefits identified at programme level may be realized, as illustrated in Figure 5.5.

The Business Programme at the right of the diagram shows a forecast cost of $4,028,750, spread across a combination of BAU activity and two projects (IT and Property). For this investment, the

FIGURE 5.5

IT PROJECT

PSG: D Dimmock, P Proctor, F Agnew

Project Manager: S Patel

Code	Item	Cost	Income
x345a	xxx Proj IT	50,000	99,322
x345b	xxx Proj S-C	49,322	0
		99,322	99,322
		0	

PROPERTY PROJECT

PSG: A Brown, S Saunton, A Hall

Project Manager: R Huppert

Code	Item	Cost	Income
x523	xxx Project	1,643,214	1,643,214
		1,643,214	1,643,214
		0	

BUSINESS PROGRAMME

Sponsors: G Bennett, E Smith, G Painton

Manager: K Gordon

Code	Item	Cost	Income
	BAU	2,286,214	7,300,000
x345	IT	99,322	7,300,000
x523	Property	1,643,214	
		4,028,750	7,300,000
		3,271,250	

SUBCONTRACTOR PROJECT

PSG: F Street, E Baines, C Underwood

Project Manager: B Billingham

Code	Item	Cost	Income
x345b1	xxx Proj Ph1	11,822	49,322
x345b2	xxx Proj Ph2	12,000	
x345b3	xxx Proj Ph3	15,500	
x345b4	xxx Proj Ph4	10,000	
		49,322	49,322
		0	

Summary
3,271,250

programme forecasts a projected income of $7,300,000. On balance, this suggests a margin of $3,271,250, a figure which is summarized in the stand-alone box.

The IT and Property projects to the left of the Business Project are breaking even. That is, the amount they forecast to spend is exactly balanced by the budget they have been granted by the programme. Furthermore, the Subcontractor Project is showing a similar break-even. It has received its budget from the IT Project and is not expected to overspend its allowance. In other words, although the projects are expected to deliver benefits that outweigh the investment being made in them, the benefit is identified at programme level. Thus, when incentivizing people involved in projects of this nature, a different approach is needed. Rather than rewarding them when the benefits are achieved (which in the case of a programme may be many years hence), it may be more effective to reward their ability to contain costs or produce 'quality' deliverables on time. The programme must take care of the benefits management, not the projects themselves.

Do not leave the realization of benefits to chance

Benefits Realization is a period which follows the closure of the project and during which the benefits intended from the project are expected to gather. The objective of the Benefits Realization period is to ensure that the benefits outweigh the investment, according to the targets outlined in the Business Case. The governance put in place for the project will have been removed during the Project Closure stage and in any case would be unnecessary and inappropriate for the activities which lie ahead. So in order to achieve what might be considered a successful Benefits Realization period, the following questions must be addressed:

- What responsibilities must be assigned during the Benefits Realization period, and to whom?
- How may the growing costs and benefits be monitored, measured and controlled?

- When can the Benefits Realization period come to an end?
- How will the organization reward success or failure?
- Can the benefits be shown to have made a contribution to the wider change agenda?

Roles and responsibilities

Since it was they who first commissioned the project, the CMT has ultimate responsibility both for a successful conclusion to the period, and for the realization of benefits that sufficiently outweigh the investment. It is also responsible for commissioning projects which contribute to the strategic growth and development of the organization. Therefore, although the sponsor promoted the project and persuaded others to follow, it was the CMT who considered it a sufficiently worthwhile venture to merit an investment of their organization's money.

As the organization looks for the benefits to be realized, the sponsor may be considered the CMT's direct report. Whilst they will commonly have a 'line' role to which they are required to return, the sponsor has additional responsibility to monitor, measure and control the mounting costs and benefits during this period. To do so may require some support. Many organizations provide assistance to the sponsor at this time, perhaps in the form of someone who has the expertise and time to take on a monitoring and measuring role. Whether or not the sponsor remains intimately involved in the initiative, they must at least exercise their authority where variances in expected costs or benefits are identified. It is they alone who are expected to bring the realization of benefits back on plan.

Whether for good or ill reasons, it is not uncommon that once a project has completed, the sponsors find themselves working in an entirely different part of the organization. If it would be impractical for them to discharge their continuing responsibilities for benefits realization in light of a new role, it is crucial that someone of similar power stands in their stead. Without such an authority in place, the benefits and costs may not grow at their intended rate and the project might yet be deemed a failure.

Monitoring, measurement and control

The tracking of benefits and costs during the Benefits Realization period should be reasonably straightforward, assuming that:

- the monitoring and measurement mechanisms have been clearly enough expressed in the Business Case;
- changes to the intended benefits, costs or monitoring and measurement mechanisms have been accommodated into the Business Case during the project.

Each benefit and cost item must be separately monitored and measured. Figure 5.6 is an example of some benefits identified in a Business Case which was shown in summary in Figure 5.2.

FIGURE 5.6

Year	0	1	2	3	4
Increased revenues	0	5,000	60,000	60,000	70,000
Increased customer satisfaction	0	5,000	10,000	10,000	10,000
Competitor removal	0		20,000	20,000	20,000
Customers from new market	0		30,000	30,000	40,000
Cost savings	0	8,000	10,000	11,000	11,000
Headcount savings	0	5,000	5,000	5,000	5,000
Removal of redundant kit	0	3,000	5,000	6,000	6,000
Total	0	13,000	70,000	71,000	81,000
Cumulative total	0	13,000	83,000	154,000	235,000

In the Business Case, the Benefits Realization Plan may have looked as follows:

- Customer satisfaction is measurable before, during and after the project by means of a survey.
- A 5 per cent improvement in customer satisfaction between year 0 and year 1 is envisaged as a direct result of this project.
- In year 2, it will increase by a further 5 per cent.
- It will remain stable during years 3 and 4.
- The increase in revenue will arise from newly satisfied customers spending more on our organization's products and services as a result.

- The 5 per cent improvement in customer satisfaction will lead to an increase in sales of $5,000 in year 1, a further $5,000 in year 2, and a stabilization at $10,000 for the remainder of the whole life of the venture.
- The reduction in costs will arise from headcount savings as a result of fewer customer service personnel being required.
- The 5 per cent improvement in customer satisfaction will lead to a reduction in headcount amounting to savings of $5,000 per year, every year, for the remainder of the whole life of the venture.

Therefore, during the Benefits Realization stage, the sponsor must apply the measures described in the Benefits Realization Plan to ensure that the benefits accrue as intended. In the example above, this means that the plan must allow for:

- a survey to measure customer satisfaction commencing before the project begins, and at least every year thereafter;
- a record being taken of customer revenue commencing before the project begins, and at least every year thereafter (the management or financial reports employed should be identified here in order that there can be no misinterpretation of figures);
- a record being taken of customer service personnel headcount commencing before the project begins, and at least every year thereafter (the management or financial reports employed should be identified here in order that there can be no misinterpretation of figures);
- a record being taken of the actual operational costs of the implemented solution.

The last bullet point shows how the Benefits Realization period is just as much about monitoring and controlling the operational costs of the implemented solution as it is about managing the benefits. To fail to control costs during this period would have the same effect on the Business Case as if the benefits failed to mount: the margin, or difference between costs and benefits, would be reduced.

Conclusion

The use of a Business Case to confirm or challenge the viability of a project may be seen by some as an inconvenience. Yet if a project is recognized as one of a range of investment opportunities, its purpose becomes crucial. This is the mindset that must exist in any environment where money is invested in projects. Those who worry that the Business Case may expose a flaw in their proposal should recognize that theirs is but one initiative which seeks to move the organization forward. Should the project fail to stand up to the intense scrutiny to which a Business Case will expose it, the good of the wider institution will have been served. Whether the initiative is curtailed or sponsored actually matters less than that the decision is made after a thorough assessment of a robust Business Case.

SUMMARY

- Commercial expectations must first be clearly articulated if commercial success is to be measured and realized.
- The management of benefits is of equal importance to the management of costs.
- The Business Case is the only expression which describes the change being sought and therefore has a life which extends beyond the project itself.
- The Business Case can be used as a tool to promote the project, and to challenge it.
- Commercially quantifiable benefits matter most – the rest is conversation.
- Business cases may be used to consider not only the merits and risks of an individual project but also the comparative values of several.
- An initiation process adds essential discipline to what might otherwise be a journey fuelled purely by emotion.
- By revealing the interdependencies of projects, business cases help to scope, separate and join projects.
- The realization of benefits happens during a post-project period during which the attention and commitment of the sponsor are crucial to embed the promised change.

CHAPTER SIX

ACCEPT THAT THINGS WILL CHANGE

This chapter covers:

- the importance of accepting that there will be a continuous pressure on an organization's projects to change;
- the means by which scope may be defined, agreed and managed;
- the value of contingency as a means of funding necessary changes to projects;
- the need for a simple yet robust change management system to allow effective decision making;
- the way in which the change management system must be used to challenge requests for projects to change, rather than to provide a route for their unqualified acceptance.

When so much time and effort may have been invested in defining and describing a project – and in getting the funding and schedule to deliver it – it is not surprising that there may be a reluctance to countenance any changes to its purpose, scope or plan. Although such thoughts may be understandable, they are unrealistic because change – the very thing which prompted the need for a project in the first place – will be an unrelenting pressure throughout its lifetime. Failing to accommodate, or even consider, the need for change can result in projects which are out of date, poorly focused or irrelevant. So although the careful management of a project is crucial from the moment it is conceived, control should not be so severe that:

> *Myth 6: Nothing can be allowed to change.*

In this chapter, a light will be shone on the value and practice of estimating, planning and controlling changes to projects.

CASE STUDY

A respected logistics provider sought to introduce what was then a revolutionary innovation. Customers who had previously had only the option of purchasing their storage and delivery services over the phone or at warehouses would instead be able to do so online.

It was known that this was a crucial development which would give the organization a vital lead over its competitors; it would be a race to the finish and the organization wanted to be sure that it was first across the line. To begin with, enthusiasm was high and there was a commitment across the business, and across the board. The innovation was of huge importance, and so too was the protection of what was already a major revenue stream for the business. Given that so much depended on the service, a great deal of money had been provisioned for the project; the amount was so big that it was impossible to believe it would not be sufficient.

That so much had been made available to the project suggested to those who administered spending that there would always be enough. Even though the money was provided in smaller allocations, everyone knew that this was a big project and that many millions had been set aside for its completion. When a new allocation was needed, the request was made to the Project Steering Group who, usually without much challenge, provided the next block of funding. This encouraged the user community to actively participate in the specification of the solution. Although not a problem in itself, this was a state of affairs which led to the addition of several expensive features which had not been originally identified, but which slipped into scope because of their desirability amongst a limited but influential body of stakeholders.

Of course, no sum of money will last forever, and so it was with the project in question. Soon enough, someone dipped into the funding barrel and reported back that they had been able to see to the bottom. Since the intended deliverables had not yet surfaced, the diminishing pot was of enormous concern. The sponsor called for a review to be undertaken which would explain where the money had been spent, and how it had come to be used so quickly.

When the review completed, its conclusions were relatively simple: there was an inadequate statement of requirements, too little financial control had been put in place, and more changes than expected had been encountered. The sponsor responded with two specific measures. The first was to put in place a set of financial controls which required his signature to authorize any expense above a relatively small amount. Although draconian, it was an understandable reaction given that appropriate controls had been absent 'on his watch'. Secondly, he announced that further, limited funds had been made available on condition from the board of directors that there was to be 'zero contingency'.

The project entered its second, more austere stage, during which the purse strings were watched avidly. The controls allowed for the better management of the project's finances, but tremendous delays were incurred as nearly every expense had to pass across the sponsor's desk. And since there was still no stable set of requirements, he was faced with the additional task of having to discern what was in or out of scope. So it was unsurprising that not before long, rumours began to circulate of a competitor who would soon be in a position to launch their own service first. But worse still was the revelation that they would be including a specific, additional feature: real-time tracking.

This killer innovation would allow customers to track the movement of their goods around the country simply by logging on to their online account. At the time, this was such a mould-breaking development that its presence in a rival's proposition threatened to put at risk the organization's future viability. A buzz of nervous concern spread throughout the project. The Project Manager responded to a request from the users by composing a report which made the case for a further release of additional cash to allow for the organization to add a real-time tracking service to the project's scope.

The sponsor took the argument to the board of directors, the group who had earlier asserted that there was to be zero contingency. He found their statement to be true: all available funds had been fully committed to projects across the organization and there was nothing left to buy the business out of its present predicament.

And the project might have ended there had the potential consequences for the entire business not been quite so stark. Upon realizing what impact their rival's real-time tracking facility might have on their own competitive position, the board halted several less-critical projects and released sufficient funds to accommodate the functionality into their own project. Combined with the tighter financial management and a revised, diminished scope, the project enabled them to deliver a competitive offering which was released to the market without too much further delay, and which allowed them to maintain and grow their business, narrowly avoiding what might otherwise have been a catastrophe.

What this means

Change is inevitable

There is barely a single project that has completed in exactly the way it was planned. In the Case study project, if the need to change had not been inspired by a competitor, it is likely that it would have come from elsewhere. On realizing that change had already eaten into their budget, the organization responded by putting in place some controls. Although sensible, the controls said much about their cultural attitude: the measures they put in place sought to prevent change rather than to manage it. The board's assertion that there was to be 'zero contingency' offered an insight into their mentality. By removing any contingency, they disabled the business from responding to one of its most basic pressures, change.

The scope must be nailed down

The requirements were insufficiently defined and were not agreed. Without a baseline against which to measure the impact of change, it became almost impossible to know what effect any change request might have on the project. Since the scope was fluid, it was never possible to know whether the money was being spent responsibly or not. The sponsor responded by nailing down the only thing he knew how to control – the budget – but not the requirements. This resulted in every request being judged only on whether it was affordable, but not on whether it had any merit, usefulness or realistic chance of being implemented.

Change can have consequences for the project

Change exerted its influence across every measure of the project. The pressure placed on the budgets led to the timescales becoming challenged. As noted above, the scope and quality of the deliverables were contested, and the benefits – the very reason behind the project – were called into question.

Change can have consequences for the portfolio

The consequences of change were not limited to the project alone. Since there had been no specific contingency pot set aside, the board of directors, acting in the capacity of a Change Management Team, were forced to sacrifice several other projects in order to save the one they considered to be the business's priority.

Change has many sources

Some of the earlier changes to impact the project were entirely self-imposed. They were choices which the organization had themselves identified and decided to accept. Later, the project faced an unanticipated challenge from outside the business in the form of the competitor's real-time tracking functionality.

Change must be managed

Regardless of from which source the changes originated, the organization had no management in place to anticipate, capture, assess and act upon them. Some management measures were put in place by the sponsor when he realized that the budget had not been adequately controlled, but the way in which he did so had two detrimental effects. Firstly, it assumed that cost was the only consequence of change which required especially tight management, resulting in a failure to consider the impact elsewhere. Secondly, it assumed that a single control point in the whole process – himself – would be enough to facilitate effective management. This resulted in the absence of anything but a commercial perspective being brought to bear on any change management decisions; the specialist and user perspectives were almost completely excluded from the process.

Change can be anticipated

The organization's only recognition of the need to manage change during the project was to allocate a huge budget, assuming that it would be sufficient to mitigate any challenge they might face. Yet without any foreknowledge of the potential volume, complexity or urgency of the changes, there was no correlation between the budget they had set aside and what they might actually need. The culture in place was focused too much on dealing with problems when they arose, rather than anticipating and planning for them, a characteristic which will be covered further in Chapter 10.

The consequences of ignoring the imperative

If an organization believes that projects must resist change, or should be impervious to it, they will face serious consequences. First, the deliverables arising from their projects will be less able to satisfy the real needs of the users. Second, by pursuing objectives which have become either irrelevant or misplaced, they will spend more than they need. And third, they will fail to keep pace with the changing world around them and see their more fleet-footed competitors benefit first.

The crucial message to such organizations is not that they should accommodate changes without a care, but that they should have in place a culture and practices which allow for balanced consideration of the consequences of change on the project.

The solutions

Deliver incremental change

Many projects grow out of control because they take on too much. There are great benefits in building a programme of much smaller projects, each of which has a greater chance of delivering something quickly which swiftly realizes its benefits. In the context of managing change, such projects are less likely to become out of date too quickly, and stand a greater chance of delivering before the world overtakes them.

Establish a baseline

A baseline is an authorized record of a project variable at a specific point in time. Amongst others, a baseline may be set for the project's timescale, budget, scope or benefits. Setting a baseline is like taking a date-stamped photograph of the project. It shows what the project looked like at a point in time – what it was expected to cost, when it was due to deliver, what it would produce, what value it would confer on the organization, and so forth. A great benefit of a baseline is to allow for the consequence of a change to be assessed in order that a decision can be made to accept it or not. Without a baseline, it becomes impossible to know what impact a change may have on any of the project's variables, resulting in either a reluctance to accept any change at all, or the accommodation of changes without knowledge of the consequence.

One of the reasons why Project Managers place such great importance on obtaining approval of the Project Plan and Business Case at the outset is because the Project Steering Group's acceptance of them transforms the documents into the baseline against which success will be measured. Whenever a request to change the project is encountered, for whatever reason and from whomsoever it may originate, an assessment may be carried out to understand its impact on the Project Plan and Business Case. If any of the baseline measures look to be impacted in any serious way, the Project Manager may seek the Project Steering Group's approval to have them changed, or 're-baselined'.

It follows that each of the variables must be measurable. In this respect, timescale and budget are relatively straightforward to determine: a date on a calendar or a financial value serves well. Subject to the guidance provided in the previous chapter, it is also relatively easy to quantify benefits. The greatest challenge comes when attempting to measure the quality and scope of the deliverables expected from the project. This is such a significant challenge that the whole of the next chapter is devoted to the topic.

Of course, there are ways of baselining a project without first defining the scope and quality of its deliverables. It is entirely possible to state a sum of money and request that what is delivered never exceeds that budget. Alternatively, time may be of the essence, in which case the users will receive what has been developed when the clock stops. Neither is unheard of, yet it is worth considering this: once the budget and time have been exhausted, the sole remaining legacy of a project is the deliverable it has produced. For that reason alone, it is worth baselining the quality and scope of the deliverables first such that it is easier to negotiate the time and cost required to produce them. This way, quality gets a look in from the outset, and the impact of change can be measured against it.

In Chapters 4 and 5, I made the case for creating a set of project success criteria for which time, cost and benefits were all candidates. In addition to these relatively simple measures, users frequently expect that their 'requirements' must be met. A Requirements Specification is a document in which their needs are commonly captured, articulated and baselined. Each requirement must be described as clearly and substantially as possible since it is against such statements that any possible changes will be compared. Changes may take the form of entirely new requirements (such as the need for real-time tracking described in the Case study), those which are no longer needed, or variations of existing ones. When expressing requirements, it may be helpful to capture them in the form shown in Figure 6.1.

The fields identified in the form are as described here:

- Item: unique identifying number for the requirement.
- Source: the person, meeting or deliverable from which the requirement was identified.
- Priority:
  - Essential: the solution is unacceptable without this requirement satisfied;
  - Desirable: the solution should meet this requirement, but would not be unacceptable without it;
  - Optional: if a solution is possible, it will be accepted, but is not necessary.
- Description: textual description of the requirement.
- Owner: the person to whom ownership of the requirement has been assigned.
- Acceptance criteria: the measures to be used when determining the solution's fitness for purpose.
- Supplier: the person or body who has been assigned the task of developing a solution.
- Complexity: the relative difficulty of developing a solution:
  - Low: the solution (or similar) has been developed before and presents no challenge;

FIGURE 6.1

Item	Source	Priority	Description	Owner	Acceptance criteria	Supplier	Complexity	Cost
1	User Needs Workshop	Essential	20 customer service staff to have been trained in the use of the system	User authority	All trained staff can use the system as intended, unsupervised	Training Division	Medium	3,500
2	User Needs Workshop	Desirable	Client's purchase history retained and available in real time	User authority	Client purchase history is always available, and is accurate	IT Division	Desirable	1,000
3	User authority	Optional	Interface into CRM system to allow nightly synchronization of customer name and address details	User authority	Customer name and address details are never more than one day out of sync	IT Division	Medium	7,000

- Medium: the solution (or similar) may have been developed before but requires bespoke elements;
- High: the solution has not been developed before and will require a bespoke approach.

● Cost: the estimated person-day and/or materials cost of developing the solution.

Having an explicit and baselined statement of requirements allows for the management of the quality and scope of the project's deliverables, especially when a request is made to change either measure. However, since the timescale and budget for the project will, to a large extent, have been based on an understanding of the statement of requirements, any changes to those requirements are likely to have an impact on the project's timescale, budget or both. It will serve everyone well to have anticipated what volume and scale of change are to be expected.

Anticipate change

Change is inevitable, and a good proportion of it will be justifiable too. It follows that in order to accommodate justifiable change, time and a budget must be set aside to pay for it. This pot is what is called 'contingency', a fund of time and/or budget which allows for changes to be accommodated. There are, broadly speaking, four things for which it will be used:

● mitigating risks: providing the funds to pay for a solution if an anticipated obstacle is encountered;
● resolving issues: paying for the solution to unanticipated problems which have to be resolved for the project's benefits to remain achievable;
● allowing changes: providing the funds to accommodate new opportunities into the scope of the project;
● impact assessment: paying for the time and effort required to assess any of the three items above such that a solution may be identified and proposed.

For any contingency to be sufficient suggests that it must have been soundly estimated. This begs the question: who does the estimating? Ideally, everyone involved in the project should be risk aware, and thus mindful in their own plans of what contingency they will need. However, a great risk to the project's initial timescale and budget is that contingency will be added at every layer of the plan, from team member through their team leaders, Project Manager and Project Steering Group. In other words, the amounts thought necessary to manage change, issues or risks might well be double- or treble-counted. Therefore, if duplications are to be identified and removed, the contingency measures being accommodated into any part of the plan must be clearly identified.

However, this can create concern amongst those charged with project planning. They worry that if their estimates for some form of contingency are too obvious or unpalatable – or both – they will be instantly cut out. They would argue that if an amount has been proposed as a contingent measure, it is foolish to remove it without understanding why it is considered necessary, for in doing so, the mitigation for what might be a legitimate concern has been taken away. Therefore, it is crucial that senior managers act responsibly to remove this fear and instead create a culture where risks are openly discussed, change is accepted as a continuous pressure, things occasionally go wrong, and where contingency measures are considered worthy of removal only if they do not stand up to reasonable challenge. So before cutting out the contingency time or budget proposed by a Project Manager in the hope of a saving, ask first what it is specifically required to cover, and how it was estimated. Here are some techniques which may be used.

Mitigating risks

Estimating the contingency needed to mitigate risks is, actually, relatively straightforward. Having identified the risks (see Chapter 10), one or more mitigations may be identified for each. It is these that will cost the project if they are enacted, the sum of such costs becoming a part of the contingency pot. For example, the risk that a supplier may fail to deliver on time might be mitigated by placing an alternative yet more expensive supplier in readiness. The difference in cost is the amount which may be set aside as contingency. An alternative mitigation may be to build in an additional two weeks' duration to the project in anticipation of the supplier's delay. As the potential delay will also have a likely impact on the project's budget, it would be sensible to account for a contingency of additional time and cost.

Since risks are, by definition, yet to happen, it is possible that senior managers may feel uncomfortable setting aside a budget of time and money for something which may not arise. Therefore, it is possible to adjust the contingency according to the likelihood of its being needed. For instance, if it is thought that there is a 20 per cent likelihood of the supplier delivering late, the money being sought in contingency might be reduced to 20 per cent of the full amount needed. However, this way of managing contingency carries a serious consequence: the total contingency pot would be insufficient if all risks were to be realized at one time. And since the estimated likelihood of any one risk materializing may change over time, the contingency pot – and the risks which require mitigation – must be dynamically managed. So as the initial estimates of the likelihood of each risk may increase or decrease as more becomes known about the project, there should be a consequent effect on the contingency. For example, if the likelihood of the supplier risk described above looks to be creeping upwards from 20 per cent to, say, 80 per cent, it would make great sense to seek additional contingency, or to increase the proportion of the existing contingency pot set aside for its mitigation.

Resolving issues and allowing changes

Since issues are, by definition, those things which we have failed to anticipate, it is not easy to estimate what amount of contingency may be needed to tackle them. The same may be said of changes which, on identifying them, seem quite reasonable yet which were not included in the original scope. This is where it may be helpful to consider the general 'riskiness' of the project. Consider the following questions:

- Impact on business as usual:
  - Is the Benefits Realization phase likely to last long?
  - Will the project significantly affect the organization's business-as-usual commitments, especially sales and operations?
  - Are any working practices expected to change as a result of the project?
  - Are people's roles and responsibilities likely to change?
- Stability of requirements:
  - Is the current burden of change within the business area already high?
  - Is there a history of changing requirements in this business area?
  - Is the business area subject to external regulation?
- Governance:
  - Will a systemized approach to the management of the project be difficult to apply?
  - Will a systemized approach to the development of any IT components be difficult to apply?
  - Will structured requirements-gathering and approval procedures be challenging to undertake?
- People:
  - Is there a difference amongst senior executives regarding their commitment to this project?
  - Are the developers and users likely to have difficulty working in partnership?
  - Are those involved in the project relatively inexperienced in the values and practices of the organization?
  - Is easy access to experienced technical competences likely to be a challenge?
- Novelty:
  - Is this the first time anything similar has been undertaken by the organization?
- Complexity and size:
  - Will a significant number of customers or users be involved in the project?

- Will any external suppliers be needed?
- Will there be interdependencies between this project and any others?
- Does this project represent a complex technological change?
- Is the project likely to take longer than a year?

Twenty questions are listed. If all 20 are answered 'yes', it suggests that the project is likely to run into a significant number of issues or changes. Perhaps a contingency amount equal to one-fifth of that set aside for risk mitigation should be added. If half of the questions are answered 'yes', the amount added might be one-tenth of that set aside for mitigating risks. In other words, the estimates are imprecise, but they are at least based on some form of reasoning. An alternative (or additional) technique might be to consider previous, similar projects and assign an amount of contingency based upon knowing by how much their final duration and costs varied from their initial estimates.

Changes, as opposed to issues, are those things which may not have been anticipated, yet cannot strictly be considered a problem. If they look to be exceptional, consider justifying them in their own right by means of a Business Case or postponing them to a later release of the solution.

Impact assessment

If the volume of change – or of Change Requests – is likely to be high, it is probable that a number of the project's valuable people will spend a good deal of their time understanding the problem or opportunity, identifying a solution, assessing its impact and developing a plan. Not only might this otherwise become an unplanned drain on the project, but it will also divert their energy and expertise from the parts of the project in which they are meant to be engaged. The contingency pot should also include an amount to pay for the administration and management of change, not only the changes themselves. A sum of at least two to three person-days might be set aside for each Issue or Change Request which is encountered. It needs only that the estimated number of Issues or Change Requests get into double figures for the cost of change administration and management to become a significant burden.

Be sure that anyone who requests a change is also required to justify the drawing down of contingency funds for the assessment needed, otherwise there will be no barrier to an organization's enthusiasm to grow the project one change at a time!

Use a process to manage changes

Without adequate governance in place, a project can quickly lose focus on what should and should not be in its scope. A simple but strict change management process should be put in place. Figure 6.2 is an example of how it might appear.

FIGURE 6.2

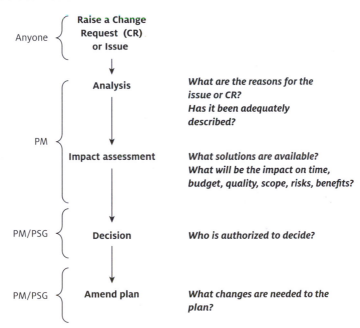

Anyone {	**Raise a Change Request (CR) or Issue**
PM {	**Analysis** — *What are the reasons for the issue or CR? Has it been adequately described?*
	Impact assessment — *What solutions are available? What will be the impact on time, budget, quality, scope, risks, benefits?*
PM/PSG {	**Decision** — *Who is authorized to decide?*
PM/PSG {	**Amend plan** — *What changes are needed to the plan?*

Raise a Change Request (CR) or Issue

Anyone may raise a CR or Issue; it is better to know of a problem or opportunity. The details may be captured in a simple pro-forma.

Analysis

The CR or Issue is scrutinized to ensure that the cause is adequately described, and any identified consequences are understood. Since the pro-forma will become the principal record, it is important that it remains as complete and as accurate as possible at each stage of its completion.

Impact assessment

The CR or Issue is considered to determine what the effect of its solution may be on the project's timescale, budget, quality, scope, risk profile and benefits. It should not be assumed that the project will always be detrimentally affected by a change; the impact may be very positive, saving the organization from unnecessary expense or providing an otherwise unnoticed opportunity for growth and development.

There may be more than one option available to address the CR or Issue, in which case a recommendation should be sought. Doing nothing may be one possibility, the impact of which should be also assessed.

If the project is already constrained by a fixed deadline, budget or scope, the options are reduced further:

- to accommodate a change while keeping to a fixed deadline:
  - more resources may be necessary;
  - faster resources may be needed;
  - quality and/or quality checks may have to be reduced;
  - the scope of what is delivered may have to be reduced;
  - overtime/weekend work may have to be increased;
  - holidays may have to be cancelled.
- to accommodate a change while working within a fixed budget:
  - cheaper resources may be required;
  - fewer resources may be employed;

- quality and/or quality checks may have to be reduced;
- the scope of what is delivered may have to be reduced;
- delivery dates may have to be delayed;
- overtime/weekend work may have to be reduced;
- holidays may have to be cancelled.
- to accommodate a change while meeting the original quality and content expectations:
  - more resources may be necessary;
  - 'better' resources may be needed;
  - quality processes, including tests, may have to be improved;
  - customer expectations may have to be better managed;
  - delivery dates may have to be delayed;
  - discounts may have to be offered;
  - some components may have to be deferred until later.

In all cases, further but stark options include:

- delivering late;
- delivering over budget;
- delivering lower quality or reduced scope;
- if the Business Case is compromised, cancelling the project.

Decision

The Project Manager has a more limited level of authority than the Project Steering Group. Which of them decides depends entirely upon the extent of the impact the solution may have. The concept and practice of 'escalation conditions' were described in Chapter 3, and are repeated here:

> *The Project Steering Group provides its Project Manager with a degree of time and budgetary flexibility so that he or she may act on their own authority within pre-agreed constraints. So if the escalation conditions for time and cost have been set for ±two weeks and ±5 per cent respectively, the Project Steering Group need not be involved in or troubled by the daily management of the project as long as its forecast end date does not vary by more or less than two weeks and the forecast cost remains within ±5 per cent of its target. If at any time the Project Manager forecasts that the project will not*

be completed within the agreed escalation conditions, the problem must be escalated immediately to the Project Steering Group for a decision on how to proceed as the Project Manager's boundaries of authority have been breached. Crucially, escalation conditions do not mean that the Project Steering Group is allowing their Project Manager to overspend or deliver late. The conditions provide the flexibility which the Project Manager will need to allow their daily management of the project to continue unhindered, whilst underlining the Project Steering Group's power to act if the project should be forecast to veer too far off track.

So these same rules may be used to determine which of the Project Manager or Project Steering Group is authorized to decide on the outcome of a Change Request or Issue.

In any case, the contingency pot should not be at the general disposal of the Project Manager, but instead kept aside under the control of the Project Steering Group. When mitigations are needed, or when Issues and Change Requests are encountered which require the decision to be escalated, the Project Manager uses the change management process to request some of what has been set aside as contingency. In this way, control is retained by the senior-most authority in the project for what might be a substantial amount of money.

Apply change management practices across all projects

As the Case study illustrated, the accommodation of change in a single project may have an effect on projects elsewhere in the portfolio. It follows that the Project Steering Group might use similar escalation conditions to raise matters for the Change Management Team's attention, so the CMT may also need to enact contingency measures of their own.

Conclusion

It is good that, in many organizations, people appear to accept that change is inevitable. This is perhaps why the discipline of project management is growing ever more widespread. However, an acceptance of change without challenge will lead to unexpected outcomes. That someone senior has demanded a modification to a project should not mean that its consequences should not be known. So, like the organizations which created them, projects must be ordered about the way in which they respond to the continuous pressure to change. It is only in this way that projects can stay sufficiently ahead of the world around them and deliver the positive transformation we expect.

SUMMARY

- If progress is to be managed, a baseline must be created against which the consequences of changes may be measured.
- To maximize the project's chances of staying ahead of the world around it, consider re-scoping its breadth and ambition – it may be better to have two swifter, smaller projects which each deliver less, than a larger one which fails to move with the times.
- Anticipate change so that you are better prepared when it arrives.
- The sources of requests or demands to change a project are varied – encourage people to embrace the need for change, but be sure that there are mechanisms in place to capture and challenge their requests.
- Projects are rarely isolated – ensure that the dependencies between projects are understood so that the consequences of change of one on another can be understood.
- Adopt, grow and reward a risk-focused, change-disciplined mindset.

CHAPTER SEVEN

MANAGE PRODUCTIVITY, NOT ACTIVITY

This chapter covers:

- the importance and practice of planning and producing deliverables which meet a specified standard;
- the need to manage efficient work.

There's something about being busy that feels good. For many people, the buzz that comes from hard work and industry can be a reward in itself. Yet we invest in projects not to keep people active, but to produce deliverables which, when used, lead to the realization of benefits.

'Productivity' is too often considered to mean 'efficiency'. With projects particularly in mind, such an opinion is entirely inadequate. Productivity is the discipline of producing deliverables in an efficient way to a defined and agreed standard. So it is a myth to believe that:

Myth 7: Activity equals productivity.

This chapter will consider how we can most efficiently specify, plan, construct, test and hand over the deliverables which meet the needs of the project's stakeholders.

CASE STUDY

Thinking itself perceived as a little tired and behind the times, a large organization decided to redevelop its website. The director of IT was appointed as the sponsor and given a reasonable sum of money which, he was instructed, was to help the organization convey to its customers a more 'dynamic profile'.

His in-house IT development team was to be engaged in the project. This would not only allow for the solution to be built more economically than if it were put out to tender, but also promised a more intimate relationship with those members of the marketing department who were charged with specifying the requirements. As the project had been characterized from the outset as being 'technical', a Project Manager was selected from the IT development team. She developed a plan which, from her specialist perspective, allowed for the usual stages to be progressively delivered. There was time set aside for gathering the requirements, designing a solution, developing the website, testing it and, in three months' time, implementing it.

A month into the project, the managing director was leaving his office one evening, and saw a glow coming from a room at the end of the corridor. On inspection, he found five members of the marketing team in heated discussion around what was displayed on a computer screen. Struck by their dedication at this late hour, he told them to order pizzas and the next day mentioned at a board meeting how impressed he was with the hard work and commitment being invested into the project. He sent an instruction that an account should be set up with the local pizza restaurant, and that anyone working on the project after seven o'clock should be allowed to order an evening meal.

What he did not know was that the same team of five people had been working at that pace since the project began, and had been unable to agree a set of requirements. On that particular evening, and for two days prior, they had been deliberating whether the company's logo should appear in the upper left- or right-hand side of the screen.

The Project Manager did not share the managing director's enthusiasm for the marketing team's commitment. The timeline showed a period of two weeks allocated to the gathering of requirements which had overrun by at least as much again, and showed no indication of completion. She saw her plan becoming less and less achievable as the days (and nights) progressed. She took her concerns to the director of marketing. His response disappointed her. Expressing requirements was a difficult and challenging process with which the team was unfamiliar; his people were giving their all to the project and deserved some thanks and encouragement. He would only sign off their work when he felt that 'all the issues had been covered'.

Yet the Project Manager's frustration lay not only in the team's inability to complete the task on time, but in the inefficiencies she witnessed. She might have been able to understand a slipping deadline had it been down only to the complexity of the task, as suggested by the director of marketing. But whenever she sought to speak with the team, they were engaged in all manner of activity which was unrelated to the project.

Then, momentously, the marketing team announced that they had completed the requirements-gathering stage, and were ready to hand over to the IT designers. That the timeline for the project had now slipped by half of its planned duration was of manageable consequence; it was a relief to know that a project stage had ended. Yet when the IT designers took a look at the list of requirements, they found them to be written in such a way as to be almost indecipherable. As a series of lengthy paragraphs, they were not in a format which could be translated into a design, nor was there any suggestion as to what priority each requirement carried. When it came to testing the eventual solution, the statements would not be able to serve adequately as a measure of fitness. And the Project Manager was frustrated that she was unable to find any data within the document that would help her to get a sense of the scope and size of the work ahead from which to refine earlier estimates of timescale and cost.

The IT design team insisted that, whilst the documented output from the requirements-gathering stage might suit the needs of the marketing department in expressing their wishes, it failed to meet their own demand for a 'catalogue of needs'. The director of IT weighed in to support their assertion that there was no alternative but to rework the document into something more structured which could better suit the needs of the widening readership. Amongst the marketing team, there was an almost audible sigh of discontent for which no amount of pizza would ever compensate.

The project struggled to a badly delayed completion date and was greeted by all of those who had participated not with satisfaction but with relief. The 'dynamic profile' the organization was so keen to promote to the world outside was by now much harder to locate inside the business. And when the managing director announced the next 'exciting project', significantly fewer participants volunteered themselves, despite the promise of a nightly all-you-can-eat buffet.

What this means

Clearly define success

Chapter 4 explained the importance of defining a clear vision for the project. The oversimplified instruction to redevelop the website so that it might convey a more dynamic profile was bound to lead to confusion and misinterpretation. How exactly was anyone supposed to translate such a subjective statement into a set of deliverables?

Engage and incorporate the most suitable stakeholders

Chapter 3 described the value of treating a project as a vehicle in which a diverse range of people might participate and benefit. In this example, the confusion concerning the vision was further compounded by assuming that this was 'an IT project'. This resulted in the project falling within the management remit of the IT department, rather than being seen as a shared endeavour. As a result, the plans were drawn up and approved by people who understood technology projects, but who were less able to translate the very superficial vision into a robust and reliable schedule of work. The benefits expected from a close working relationship between the IT and marketing departments were not realized as, perhaps, each assumed the other would know what was required of them.

A project must produce deliverables

A successful project is a temporary management environment created to produce a specified deliverable which, when used, leads to benefits which outweigh the investment made in its development and operation. A project might be divided into stages with each producing its own 'specified deliverable'. The Case study project was sensibly split into several stages, but it was apparent from the conduct of the requirements-gathering segment that no clear deliverables had been specified. As a result, not only was the delegation of work to the marketing team made more difficult, but nor was it possible to plan or measure confidently when the stage might complete; essentially, requirements gathering would stop when the time ran out. And it is hard to know how the Project Manager had determined how much time was needed without having defined the deliverable. In the face of such an uncertain plan, the Project Manager could never reliably appraise the director of marketing of the consequences of his delayed approval.

A further consequence of failing to describe what was expected from the requirements-gathering stage was that no one really got from it what they needed. The output produced by the marketing team failed to serve the needs of the IT design team who depended on it as an input to the next stage, and did not contain the information the Project Manager needed to further refine and develop the plan.

And within the stage, important decisions were not recognized as being deliverables. Since it became apparent that the position of the logo was so crucial, a definitive decision should have been planned or required. In this way, it could have been treated as a measurable milestone, and managed authoritatively.

Do not confuse activity with productivity

The managing director was mightily impressed that people were working into the night. But without sufficient understanding of the project, he mistook hard work for fruitful work and further compounded the problem by rewarding poor productivity with pizza.

The Project Manager was concerned that, despite their nocturnal efforts, the marketing team was not focused on project-related work when she called on them. This may have been legitimate, but suggests that she failed to account in her plans for a proportion of their time being unproductive. During these periods, they may have been engaged in business as usual, training, holidays, or any other activity which might reasonably distract them from the project.

The consequences of ignoring the imperative

The initial euphoria which sometimes arises from periods of intense work does not last. Sickness and burnout result, placing a greater burden on those who remain. Such furious activity becomes part of the culture and is sometimes worn as a badge of pride; productivity is assumed to correlate to how many hours workers spend at their desks. Too little emphasis is placed on what they produce. Plans fail to account for deliverables and become ever more unachievable as estimates are harder to make. Senior managers who oversee and approve of such a culture reward inefficient or non-productive behaviour. This only perpetuates it further.

Time, a most precious commodity, is used poorly, leading to rising costs and poor quality. Only those who have no choice or who can thrive for long periods on adrenaline (and pizza) will survive.

The solutions

Productivity is not just about how efficiently work is undertaken, but about what that work produces. A project's final deliverable to the organization is its legacy. How well the deliverable serves its purpose will directly affect the benefits it allows the organization to realize. So this chapter is very much focused on *quality*. Yet this is not something which can be added as an afterthought. Rather, quality can become a feature of projects which:

- allows for the more reliable estimation of timescale and budget;
- enables clearer and more effective delegation;
- enables us to know when something is complete;
- increases the likelihood of delivering what was required, first time, most times.

If organizations are to enjoy these benefits, their projects must specify, plan, construct, test and hand over deliverables which are ultimately fit for the purpose for which they were intended.

Specifying quality

In Chapter 4, consideration was given to the specification of quality for an individual project. A range of opinions was gathered from commercial, strategic, user and specialist perspectives to determine what constituted a successful outcome. These were recorded as a list of criteria which together, when prioritized, formed a vision. In this way, it is possible to say that quality has been specified for the project. That is, those who have been authorized to approve the outcome have specified their expectations.

Some of the stakeholders' expectations will relate to what happens *after* the project has completed. For instance, the sponsor will be keen to know that the benefits he was so keen to promote at the beginning of the project have eventually been delivered. But he must take a keen interest in the quality of the project's end deliverable as it will be the principal enabler of the benefits being realized.

In practice, the qualities which matter to the users and developers engaged in the project will be those that relate to the project's end deliverable, not the whole project itself.

Planning quality

Quality need not only be specified for the end deliverable. It is just as possible – and as sensible – to specify it at progressively more detailed levels. Projects can be divided into stages, each of which has a particular purpose to achieve – and a deliverable to produce. So instead of planning that a stage will complete when the time runs out, some criteria can be set against which completion can be more robustly challenged, measured and authorized. Imagine a project which has been divided into the following very high-level stages (see Figure 7.1):

- Benefits Discovery is a pre-project stage within which the idea of the project is articulated.
- Initiation is where the project is scoped, planned and structured, and seeks the authority to progress.
- Delivery is where those deliverables peculiar to the project in question are specified, constructed and tested (each of which may be considered as smaller phases within the delivery stage).
- Closure is where conditions are tested to confirm that the end deliverable may be handed over to the business-as-usual environment.
- Benefits Realization is a post-project stage within which the benefits arising from the use of the solution are achieved.

FIGURE 7.1

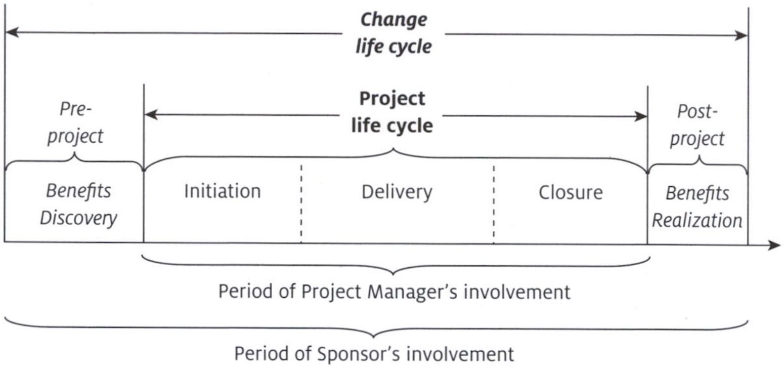

Each of the stages above should be confirmed as having been completed to a suitable standard before the next stage is commenced. But what constitutes a 'suitable standard'? Here are some suggested criteria which may be used to determine whether or not the stage can be authoritatively described as complete.

Benefits Discovery:

- Has the purpose of the potential project been adequately described?
- Has it been made clear what problem or opportunity the project is seeking to address?
- Is there an indication of what financial return on the investment may be expected from the project, should it take place?
- Has the payback period been ascertained?
- Have specific inclusions or exclusions been noted?
- Have the project's deliverables been identified?
- Has a target end date been identified?
- Has a target end budget been calculated?
- Has a next stage budget been identified?
- Have any important dates of note been listed?
- Are all assumptions reliable and trustworthy at this point in the project?

- Are all risks described in terms of their cause, their likelihood and their impact?
- Do all risks have at least one corresponding mitigation?
- Has a contingency budget been identified to provide for any identified risks or potential changes?
- Is it clear whether the project is, or isn't, mandatory?

Initiation:

- Does the Business Case show the difference over time of the costs of the project compared with its intended benefits?
- Where alternative solutions exist, does the Business Case argue in favour of a selected option?
- Is the Business Case suitable for the purposes of comparison with other projects such that the Change Management Team may prioritize across the portfolio?
- Does the Business Case consider the 'whole life' of the venture (that is, not just the project costs alone, but those which may be incurred beyond the project's eventual closure)?
- Does the Business Case suggest how a clear approval decision should be made?
- Does the Business Case clearly show the extent to which the project produces a value-adding outcome?
- Is there a clear separation of project 'ownership' from its 'daily management'?
- Is there a clearly identified, single Project Manager?
- Has each role been assigned to someone who has sufficient authority to undertake every responsibility allocated to them?
- Does the project organization as a whole contain the authority within itself to make the decisions necessary to its continued progress?
- Are all three key perspectives (commercial, user, specialist) represented on the Project Steering Group?

- Have any external clients' aspirations been accommodated?
- Have all responsibilities identified as necessary to the project been assigned to individuals?
- Have all individuals to whom roles have been assigned been acquainted with their responsibilities, and are they comfortable with them?
- Has the Project Manager been set clear escalation conditions within which to operate?
- Has a unique cost code been set for the project to which all charges can be sent?
- Does the Project Plan show how any time, cost and quality targets identified in the Business Case may be met?
- Does the Project Plan provide an internally consistent expression of how time, cost and quality expectations will be met?
- Does the Project Plan explain clearly how the project, once underway, will be kept on track?

Delivery:

- Criteria relevant to the specific nature of the project in question may be defined at a lower level. To this end, individual deliverables may be identified, each with their own detailed specification. This practice is described further at the end of this section.

Closure:

Business criteria:
- Has the project delivery team made sufficient funding provision for post-implementation support?
- Has it been made clear to the area receiving the solution that any further development work would need to be

separately scoped and budget made available in the normal manner?

- Have any relevant support departments been given responsibility to monitor and control operational spend?
- Has the period of post-implementation support been confirmed?
- Has budget been approved to cover possible bugs and fixes which may occur within the first month after closure of the project?
- Has a date been set for the first Benefit Review?
- Is it clear who will attend the Benefit Review?

User criteria:
- Does the end deliverable meet its specified quality criteria?
- Have the users and specialists finalized a Service Level Agreement, agreeing the required support service level for the solution?
- Have the required escalation procedures been negotiated?
- Has all appropriate documentation been handed over to the users?
- Have all training requirements been agreed and documented, with training plans formulated and agreed?

Specialist criteria:
- Have the specialists handed over full 'build and release' documentation?
- Have the users accepted that the solution is as expected, and that they consider it fit for purpose?
- Has the technical team executed suitable tests in an appropriate environment, and measured and documented the ability of the solution to cope with current and projected operational pressures?
- Have the specialists proven the operability of the proposed solution?
- Have all tests been fully documented and agreed, demonstrating exactly how the solution is to be implemented, and how the success of the implementation will be measured?

- Where relevant, has full documentation been provided to operations staff to monitor and administer the solution?
- Where relevant, have full details been documented and agreed before implementation planning is complete of any necessary interruptions to business, along with the length of the interruption?
- Has the impact on any interdependent functions, departments or systems been considered and have they been made aware of the project?

Realization:

- Have Benefits Reviews taken place as intended?
- Have all intended delegates participated in the Benefits Reviews?
- Have intended benefits been compared with actual benefits such that variances can be identified?
- Have variances been addressed such that they may be overcome?
- Has the opportunity been used to determine whether any additional benefits have become apparent?
- Have all benefits been commercially quantified?
- Do the benefits delivered sufficiently outweigh the investment made in the development and operation of the solution?

But what about measures of productivity during the delivery stage, that crucial period between starting and completing a project where the magic is supposed to take place? It is just as important to have a means of measuring the quantity and quality of work during this period as any other.

Where all other stages may be almost identical for every project, it is during the delivery stage that the peculiar nature of the project in question is captured. Sometimes, it is usual for the delivery stage to be broken down further and planned as a series of specialist phases, such as requirements gathering, design, build and test, but the choice of specialist phases will be very much dependent upon the nature of the project. For instance, a project to launch a new product onto the market might follow a very different development path to, say, a 'staff recruitment' project. In any case, given that the delivery stage may be an extended period, it is imperative that deliverables are planned, not just the work required to produce them.

So, the plan, in whatever form it takes, must identify the products of the work to be undertaken. Indeed, it is preferable that the deliverables are identified first, and that the activity to produce them is considered thereafter. In this way, some confidence can be gained that all activity has been geared towards producing something of use to the project.

At the very least, any plan must contain a time schedule; an expression of the dates upon which the deliverables are due to be completed. The diagram in Figure 7.2 is a simplified example of what should be expected in a deliverable-focused time schedule.

The deliverables are clearly identified to the left, the work required to deliver them appears beneath and the dependencies between the deliverable duration bars are shown as solid arrows. This schedule is telling us that the system documentation and training plan are necessary before the training materials can be produced, and that once those have been delivered to the required standard, the production of trained support staff can begin. The last three deliverables are a good example of a preferable alternative to the more traditional 'training' activity which appears in so many plans as a duration bar stretched across the schedule to an indiscriminate point in the future. The focus on the deliverables of 'training' allows us to take something which is all too easy to misinterpret, and instead describe it as a series of products which must be produced to a very specific standard in a prescribed sequence. But just how does one go about ensuring 'trained support staff' have been delivered to a suitable standard?

FIGURE 7.2

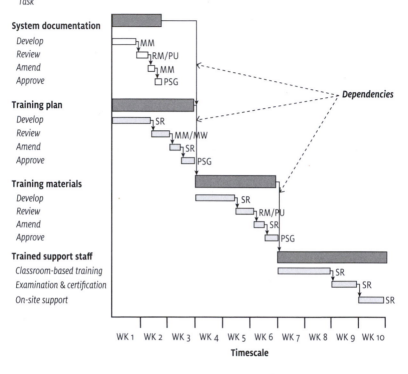

Deliverable
Task

System documentation
Develop — MM
Review — RM/PU
Amend — MM
Approve — PSG

Training plan
Develop — SR
Review — MM/MW
Amend — SR
Approve — PSG

Training materials
Develop — SR
Review — RM/PU
Amend — SR
Approve — PSG

Trained support staff
Classroom-based training — SR
Examination & certification — SR
On-site support — SR

Dependencies

WK 1 WK 2 WK 3 WK 4 WK 5 WK 6 WK 7 WK 8 WK 9 WK 10

Timescale

Figure 7.3 shows how trained support staff – the true product of their 'training' – can be articulated in a clear and measurable way. The deliverable has been described by means of the following features:

- Deliverable name – the title of the deliverable which is to be produced, and which so often remains the only thing we have to express what we know about it!
- Purpose – the reason for needing the deliverable.
- Composition – the parts from which the deliverable is formed. In the case of the example, trained support staff are people who have attained a certain level of competence via attendance on a course, examination and certification, and on-the-job support.

FIGURE 7.3

Deliverable name	Trained support staff
Purpose	To ensure that the forthcoming solution can be operated by existing support personnel
Composition	Support staff who have: 1. attended a classroom-based training course 2. been tested and certified 3. allowed access to on-site support
Quality criteria	1. Is the course material based on the most up-to-date system documentation? 2. Is the course lecturer fully conversant with the new solution? 3. Does the course last for no longer than a day? 4. Can the course cater for up to 10 people at a time? 5. Are the premises appropriate for the number of people to be trained and the style of training? 6. Have the materials been designed to cater for all levels of experience? 7. Does the examination test delegates' knowledge of each module of the course? 8. Does the examination test delegates' skill in using the solution in a range of real-life scenarios? 9. Is the on-site support provided in the form of both documented Frequently Asked Questions in addition to the presence of a knowledgeable member of the project team? 10. Will the on-site support be available 24/7 for at least the first entire month of operation? 11. After one month, are the trained support staff able to operate the new solution as required without the need for external intervention or support?

Alternatively, if a deliverable is a document, the composition might be equivalent to the table of contents, identifying the various sections which must be found within the product.

- Quality criteria – the closed questions which, when answered positively, allow an informed opinion to be exercised as to the fitness-for-purpose of the trained support staff. In other words, these are the measures which determine whether or not the deliverable has been produced to the specified standard.

Thus, in this way it is possible to plan quality at a relatively detailed level and thereby have the means by which to gain confidence that the project will be productive. In some cases, turning activities into deliverables is a straightforward matter; in others, it can be immensely challenging. For example, what might be the products of 'testing'? Some are more obvious than others. A 'test plan' might be usual, so too might be a suitable 'test environment' and some 'test data' and even some 'trained testers'. But none of these gets close to specifying the true product of 'testing'. If we were to say that the purpose of testing a newly developed computer system is to produce an error-reduced version of that system, it should be possible to define the desirable qualities of the tested system. We might do this by defining the number of unresolved, non-critical errors remaining after testing: the fewer in number, the better the quality.

The diagram in Figure 7.4 identifies three successive forms of test to be carried out on a newly developed computer system: a 'unit test', where the developers test each individual module independently, a 'system test', where the developers test the entire system, and a 'user acceptance test', where those who specified the requirements test the system to ensure that their needs have been met.

Three alternative specifications of quality are identified, represented by the lines A, B and C. Each suggests a progressively more demanding level of quality to be achieved, equivalent to the number of unresolved non-critical errors. The users who are to inherit the system might naturally wish for profile C to be pursued as they would prefer a deliverable which is as free from such errors as possible.

FIGURE 7.4

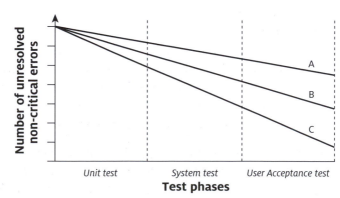

The dotted lines representing the barrier between one level of testing and the next might be thought of as 'quality gates', points past which the project should not progress until the intended standard (represented by the number of unresolved non-critical errors) has been met. However, taking account of the usual constraints of time and cost, it is possible that the investment will only allow for profiles B or A to be achieved. So it is vital that whichever profile is preferred has been clearly identified and planned for, ensuring that there is sufficient time and money to allow for the testing and refinement of quality to the desired level. The presence of such an explicit quality gate further requires that there is someone able to make the go/no-go decision. This is where the Project Steering Group must be called upon since it is their combination of commercial, user and specialist perspectives which must be brought to bear on such a key consideration.

So deliverables can only be produced to the desired standard if sufficient time and resource have been made available. Therefore, once the deliverables have been described, the time and resource needed to produce them must be estimated too. When this has been done, a plan will exist which expresses the three essential components: time, cost and quality. The Project Manager presents the plan to the Project Steering Group as a means by which the three competing imperatives might be met. If the senior managers are uncomfortable with the balance that has been struck, they are, of course, quite at liberty to require a re-plan to adjust the relative priority of time, cost and quality. So, the plan becomes the evidence which shows what can be delivered by when and for how much.

If, in addition to quality, productivity suggests efficiency, project plans must be able to show how the best use will be made of its resources. Since people are unpredictable and unique, any estimate of the effort or duration of someone's time required to develop a deliverable should take account of their different rates of efficiency. Here are some general 'rules of thumb' which can be helpful when planning:

● People will not be 100 per cent productive. If a project's estimates are to be anywhere near realistic, a contingency should be accommodated for likely non-productive time, including (at least) possible sickness, training and annual leave. Realistically, people will spend a good deal of their time managing and supervising each other. Take account of this too. Most organizations have a standard productivity rate, which can vary between 65 per cent and 80 per cent, dependent on which activities are considered to be 'non-productive' and how much allowance is estimated for each.

- Productivity does not always increase when more people are allocated to a piece of work. Indeed, the reverse can be true. For example, if I had been required to collaborate with another author in the writing of this book, it might well have taken twice as long to produce, given that we would have had to collaborate closely, manage our expectations of each other and negotiate decisions which would otherwise have been mine alone.

- People have different rates of productivity. Choosing the best person for the job, or the fastest, may not always be possible. As people work at different rates, a person's experience and speed must be a factor when creating an estimate. A junior member of the team might take two days to deliver a specific deliverable, whereas a more senior member could produce the same result in one-and-a-half days. So one should think carefully about who is to be asked to estimate the work: will it be the person who is to do the work, or someone else?

- Productivity increases are usually temporary. The American psychologist Frederick Herzberg showed that even after increasing workers' salaries, the motivational and productivity improvement lasted for a relatively short time, after which they reverted to what he called the 'Potter Line', a rate of productivity which, for them, was 'normal'. In the Case study, the inducement of pizza motivated the workforce for only a limited time.

Constructing quality

The construction of quality deliverables in an efficient manner is largely a result of having sufficiently planned quality expectations and developed estimates which take account of the realistic efficiency of the project's resources. So it is neither trite nor simplistic to suggest that building quality is relatively straightforward once it has been planned. Thereafter, instead of work or activities being delegated, Project Managers issue the instruction to produce the specified deliverables. So the language of delegation changes; 'Here's what I want you to do...' is replaced by 'Here's what I want you to deliver...'

Of course, it is essential that planned progress is controlled, so evidence of delivery must be sought on the forecast dates. Senior managers, and Project Managers, should look for proof of productivity in the form of the deliverables identified in the plan. Whether those deliverables have been produced to a sufficient standard is a matter to be confirmed through testing.

Testing quality

Testing is the means by which to determine to what extent each deliverable may be considered 'complete'. There are many different forms of test, each suitable for a particular type of deliverable:

- examination – where a physical test is necessary, for example, the means by which the 'trained support staff' in the earlier example are checked to establish the standard they have achieved, or where a computer system is put through a series of tests to identify and remove errors;
- inspection – where a product or service is scrutinized to determine its fitness, for example, a visit to the venue in which the training course is to be held;
- demonstration – where the potential errors are identified by a walk-through, for example, a module from the training course;
- formal quality review – where a group of carefully identified reviewers are invited to challenge a deliverable's ability to meet its predefined success criteria. This enables errors to be identified and corrected, for example, the proposed examination to be sat by the trainees is first scrutinized by experts;
- informal quality review – a less structured version of a formal quality review, where the product is circulated by mail or e-mail so that errors can be identified and corrected.

So productivity is not only a matter of confirming that a deliverable has been created, nor only that it has been produced efficiently, but that there is evidence of it having met the specified standard.

Handing over quality

It is not at all unusual that, at the end of the project, when little or no spare time or money remains, the quality of the deliverables being produced is questioned. This may have to do with a poor specification and planning to begin with, unsuitable construction, inadequate testing, or simply because those charged with approving the project's closure have changed their minds. Any of these may lead to users' and operators' reluctance to accept the project's deliverables. Yet, with an eye on commercial matters, the sponsor of the project may be equally reluctant to invest any more time or money in quality. Once more, it is crucial that the decision to hand over the project's deliverable to the business-as-usual environment is taken by the Project Steering Group, thereby accommodating their range of different perspectives. Its decision should be taken in light of the criteria which were earlier agreed to signify the closure of the project (see Planning quality on page 167). Significantly, this is not the point at which the success of the entire change may be judged; it will be necessary to wait until the end of the post-project Benefits Realization period to do so.

With the authority of the Project Steering Group, the Project Manager can dismantle the governance and close the project, confident that it has been a productive enterprise.

Embedding a quality-focused culture

In addition to the structured advice offered in this chapter, there are a number of further practices which can increase the likelihood of a productive project:

● Identify authoritative User authorities to participate in the Project Steering Group – they will play a crucial role in the specification, testing and approval of the project's deliverables.

- If there is a wide range of users with an interest in what the project has to produce, put in place a 'User Forum', chaired by the User authority, to manage their interests and priorities.
- Keep users involved throughout the project, or at the very least, involve business analysts as their advocates.
- Clarify and baseline requirements (with the User authority's approval) before seeking to develop a solution.
- Prototype solutions so that the quality of the deliverables may be experienced as soon as possible.
- Set clear quality gates in order that the project can be subjected to authoritative and balanced go/no-go decision points.
- Train those who will test the solution.
- Manage 'end-date' expectations to avoid compression of the testing window.
- Encourage the postponement of non-essential improvements or fixes to a future project.
- Discourage the addition or revision of non-essential features after the Requirements Specification has been approved.
- Incentivize and reward people on the production of deliverables which meet the quality standard, not just on a timely or economic completion.
- Challenge any plan which assumes its resources will operate at 100 per cent efficiency.
- Upon understanding the deliverables required, allow those who are to produce them to estimate their cost and duration for themselves.

Conclusion

No matter how vocal people may be about the importance of quality and the deliverables which enable it to be enjoyed, there is often very little evidence of productive work either in plans, or in the behaviour of project teams. So it is depressingly usual that the testing phase is where shortfalls are not only identified in the deliverable itself, but in the whole concept and practice of productive work. The mind set of so many managers remains focused on activity instead of productivity. They would rather measure how long someone spends in the office than whether they produce something of worth. Of course, the reason for this is that it is far easier to measure the movement of time or money than it is to measure a deliverable's fitness-for-purpose. But just because something is difficult, doesn't mean that it should not be done. We plan that work will be carried out in a timely and economic way; so too should we plan for it to be conducted productively.

SUMMARY

- Specify what expectations of quality exist for the project, its stages and its deliverables.
- Plan time and budget accordingly, negotiating within the project if compromises are necessary.
- Be productive, not just active, and motivate people to deliver.
- Test for the features and characteristics which were specified – do not only chase time and cost targets.
- Ensure that those who were authorized to approve the list of quality expectations are those who are held accountable for accepting the deliverables on behalf of the organization.

CHAPTER EIGHT

KEEP YOUR SUPPLIERS CLOSE

This chapter covers:

- the management of suppliers whose interests may be different from your own;
- the need for terms of engagement to be clearly and commonly understood between client and supplier;
- the importance of managing the relationship with suppliers, as well as what they deliver.

If you ask, most suppliers will tell you they have your best interests at heart. You would say the same to your own clients, and I say it to mine. Most of us mean it, yet although a project may be described as a single endeavour through which shared objectives may be met, suppliers and clients have other, fundamentally different, interests to satisfy. Although they are both seeking some measure of benefit from the project, they will each find it in a different place; the suppliers will make their money from the client who is sponsoring the project, and that client will gain their reward from the benefits the project delivers. So projects and suppliers have different shareholders to satisfy. Therefore, if different expectations are to be drawn together within the confines of the project, robust and reliable terms of engagement must be in place within the project to ensure an effective working relationship.

It is only in this way that the well-being of the project may be assured. So it is not realistic to assume that:

> *Myth 8: Our suppliers share our objectives.*

This chapter will seek to understand how supplier relationships might be better managed in order that the needs of projects are not compromised.

CASE STUDY

A highly technical project was initiated to replace a business's entire suite of computer systems. Although the organization had access to an extensive range of specialists both at home and abroad, the proposed solution was to be bought from their existing supplier and tailored according to the very specific needs of the business. The supplier had worked with the business for many years, supporting the original suite of systems which everyone now realized to be approaching the end of its natural life. So, although the business had a choice, the most obvious and acceptable solution seemed to be to continue the relationship with the existing supplier. After a consideration of alternatives, the existing incumbent was selected.

The project had been conceived by the IT department and the relationship with the supplier had always been managed through them, and so it continued. The existing contract was renewed, and was signed by the IT director and the supplier's chief executive. The IT director took up his position as Specialist authority on the Project Steering Group. The chief executive returned to his office with the great news. Both parties saw the project as the common means by which success would be achieved.

Problems arose as soon as complex technical challenges were faced. Members of the supplier's delivery team worked hard to identify some solutions. What they came up with required some interpretation; their recommendations needed to be translated into a language that the business and its users would understand. But the IT director kept the supplier at arm's length, keen to ensure they delivered according to the original plan; the last thing he wanted was to face the sponsor with a proposal for additional costs, delays and changes to the project approach. So although the supplier discovered some effective but potentially radical solutions, they never ascended far enough up the project's organization structure to reach the ears of the Project Steering Group.

As it was, the existing technical proposal was inadequate, manifested as a slipping timescale which, of course, frustrated the client. They were unsure as to the cause, and simply assumed that the supplier was not up to the task. Their suspicions led them to a full scrutiny of the contract, and it was then that their prejudices were confirmed. They discovered that the work was being undertaken on a 'time and materials' basis by which the supplier was paid for the days spent and the resources used. They took this at face value: any delay rewarded the supplier.

They investigated further. The daily rates were found to be not only far higher than anyone outside IT had imagined, but on an scale which rose in line with inflation. The client was committed to terms which seemed to disadvantage them more with every passing day.

The sponsor called the IT director and demanded to know why he had signed such a contract. The IT director explained that not only had he been told the relationship was his to manage, but that the terms were no different from those that had existed during the previous contract period. The sponsor told the IT director to solve the problem, only to be told in return that he was a technician and that commercial negotiation was surely the sponsor's job.

The bickering continued and so did the scale of the business's commercial exposure. On the one hand, it had committed to the replacement of an entire and critical suite of systems which were close to failure. On the other, it appeared to be caught in a contract which did nothing to motivate the supplier on whom the solution depended. The procurement and legal departments were engaged to discover what options might remain. The supplier mobilized its own defences since it had signed the contract in good faith and was determined to protect a revenue stream which was funding its growth overseas. Someone somewhere leaked the dispute to the trade press.

After months of wrangling, a commercial compromise was achieved which fully satisfied neither party but served to close the matter. The solution was eventually implemented so late that the supplier's contract was by then again due for renewal. Predictably, the client allowed it to lapse. Although the client's business represented a significant loss, the supplier had anticipated what seemed increasingly inevitable and had by that point invested the profits in its new venture abroad. So instead, a competitor took the prize and the head of procurement took personal responsibility for negotiating and signing the new contract.

What this means

Delivery management is not the same as relationship management

The project's senior management abdicated to the IT director their own responsibility for managing one of their most important stakeholders and risks. Project success hinged on managing the *relationship*, not merely the supplier's ability to deliver technical products according to a schedule. In pushing the supplier further away and lower into the project's organizational hierarchy, the Project Steering Group not only lessened their opportunity to manage them effectively, but diminished access to the value that the supplier might bring.

Beware of the hidden Business Case

What began as a means by which two parties might pursue a common goal was shown up to be nothing of the sort. The client had imagined that success for them both depended on the delivery of the replacement computer system. In fact, this was its own goal. For the supplier, the moment contracts were signed, success was reasonably assured. The client and supplier, although bound together by a project, had separate investors to satisfy. The client looked to the project to deliver them a cost-saving, productivity-improving, risk-averting suite of new systems. The supplier looked to the project to deliver sufficient profits to grow their own business abroad.

Operational contracts may not suit projects

Having worked reasonably successfully as a partnership for some years, the client's IT director considered the supplier worthy of a continued relationship. Yet he had seen them in only one capacity and had framed the contract around it. So although their operational support had been acceptable, the demands which a project would make on them all were very different. Where before, a timely turn-around for operational bug fixes or new releases of fault-free code might have been of the essence, what mattered during the project was access to expertise, timely and cost effective delivery of entirely new products, and a shared attitude to the project's significant risks. The existing operational contract covered no such matters.

The consequences of ignoring the imperative

Most businesses require suppliers to deliver products and services which they themselves cannot. This creates a mutual dependence which, over time, can become highly valuable to both parties. Yet, the more valuable the relationship, the greater the risks associated with its failure. Contracts and terms of reference put in place mitigations which are tailored to the nature of the risks faced by both parties. Failure to properly understand the risks of a close association in a project between a client and supplier can expose both to the effects if those risks are realized.

The solutions

Too often, the unique, risky nature of projects is misunderstood. Where two or more parties are bound together in a project environment, each pursuing its own objectives, the risk is substantially heightened. As clients subcontract work, it is inevitable that they will also lose some of the controls they would have enjoyed had the work remained 'in-house'. The possible loss of project control is the single greatest risk for a client to mitigate. Therefore, many of the solutions proposed below have to do with sharing the project's risks – and rewards – amongst the participants. This is how partnerships within projects may be developed.

From the outset of the relationship, suppliers to projects should be considered as more than just a resource pool offering only additional capacity. There is an opportunity to call upon the supplier for expertise. Although this is very difficult to plan for, commoditize and package, it remains an important contribution that is often poorly managed.

Shared risk and reward

Mutual management

Since both parties have much to be gained and lost from the initiative, it follows that the project can be the means by which both can manage the risks and rewards. I often propose that a very senior member of the supplier's commercial management team should be a member of the Project Steering Group. Many organizations' initial response is to disapprove of such a suggestion on the basis that it is their own project, not the supplier's, and that the vendor should be regarded as an important member of the delivery team, but no more. It is only when one considers the risks of treating a strategic partner in such a way that the case can be made. The Case study demonstrated how the commercial management of the supplier relationship was completely out of its control. Had the supplier's chief executive been a member of the Project Steering Group from the outset, the commercial negotiations could have been conducted within the project rather than outside it, and the subsequent upheaval avoided.

The role of a supplier on a Project Steering Group is often characterized as the specialist with the authoritative expertise borne by no one else. This may be true, but we may also require them to be the supplier's commercial authority, providing reliable decision making on a range of topics including resource availability and provision, daily rates and dispute resolution. Finding both levels of competence in one individual is often difficult, so it may be necessary to invite *two* supplier authorities to participate in the Project Steering Group: a senior manager from each of their commercial and specialist divisions. So the Case study Project Steering Group might have looked as shown in Figure 8.1.

FIGURE 8.1

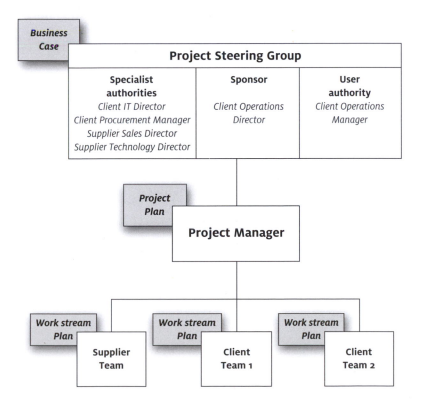

The supplier is accommodated at two levels: within the Project Steering Group, to lend the authority and expertise needed at key points throughout the project, and as a team at the delivery level, producing the specialist deliverables required by the plan.

Note how the client's procurement manager is also identified as an additional specialist authority, since the project is as dependent upon making a suitable purchase from a vendor as it is about developing a system which meets the company's needs.

Were a large number of external suppliers to be engaged, another variation on the Project Steering Group above may be to identify a 'lead supplier' through whom all others are subcontracted. By placing all vendors in the sole governance of one supplier, many risks are mitigated:

- The Project Steering Group remains a manageable size and is able to make timely decisions.
- Client access to multiple suppliers is streamlined.
- Complex specialist matters can be clearly articulated prior to consideration by the client.
- Economies can be achieved through the creation of a single contract with one supplier.

Charging models

There are, broadly speaking, three ways of paying for the services of a supplier:

Time and materials

This is the most common means of payment and presents a reasonably equitable means of remunerating the supplier for their investment in the project. However, it is worth recalling the previous chapter where the concept of productive delivery was considered, for unless the deliverable can be clearly defined and delivered, the financial impact of a delay in producing what was required lies entirely with the client.

If possible, this method of payment is best used for services which are naturally bought and sold 'by the hour' and where the deliverable is 'expertise'.

Fixed price

This method of remuneration transfers some of the risk to the supplier, discouraging them from delivering late and having the effect of sharing the hazards. To work effectively for both parties requires that the deliverables required from the supplier are clearly defined and that their fitness-for-purpose is easily measured. There is, of course, a disadvantage; when requested to share the risk, most suppliers will include a contingency to allow for any unknowns which they may face. This has the effect of increasing the fixed fee, the supplier's contingency being the insurance premium the client pays for the luxury.

A further and often overlooked drawback is that unless the quality of the deliverables has been really nailed down, the supplier may misinterpret what is required, and deliver short of what was expected. And as the previous chapter outlined, quality is not the easiest feature to describe with perfect clarity.

Shared risk and reward

This is the most sophisticated remuneration mechanism and depends from the start on the supplier and client intending to work in a close and binding partnership not just during the project but beyond. The potential rewards offered by the project are not for the enjoyment of the client alone, but for both parties to share, based on a joint commitment to the project, its risks and to the post-project operation of the end deliverable. For example, a financial services organization might develop and install its software at a discounted price on condition that they receive a percentage of the client's eventual operating profit. That the operation of the software may also result in a loss is a risk shared by both parties.

Terms of reference

From a legal perspective, the terms of reference may form a significant part of the contract since they will seek to describe what is required from the supplier, and how its delivery will be managed. They go a long way to describe the relationship which the client and supplier will have during the project. Putting aside strictly legal conditions such as confidentiality, liability limitations and so forth, robust terms of reference might seek to describe the following:

Roles and responsibilities

This will identify who is to be placed in which project roles, and what are to be their responsibilities. An attempt should be made to break through the traditional 'them and us' mindset and instead gain access to the supplier's expertise, authority and resource within the project. To this end (and as noted earlier) seek to gain a position for the supplier on the Project Steering Group in addition to their more traditional position amongst the team.

Reporting and escalation

This may be an elaboration of the relationships identified in the roles and responsibilities section above. Make clear who is reporting to whom, when, and under what conditions. This last matter helps to establish clear escalation conditions (which were described fully in Chapter 3), allowing for exceptional circumstances to be raised to the appropriate level of management for resolution.

Measures of success

It should be possible to agree upon a set of criteria which establish how the client would judge the supplier's success. The longer the list, the more demanding it will be for the supplier to satisfy the client's expectations. But a long list is not the target; rather, the list should capture what constitutes a successful relationship. Here are some examples:
- The deliverables are produced to the defined standard, on time and within the agreed budget.
- Expert opinion will be offered by the supplier without the need for an invitation from the client.
- Expert opinion will be reliable and articulated in a way which a non-specialist can understand.
- Invoices will clearly state the deliverables and services provided to the client.
- A statement of progress against plan will be available at least once a week.

This is by no means an exhaustive list; it is not difficult to conceive of more, but remember that this is a two-way relationship. The supplier may have expectations of the client. Here are some examples from their perspective:

- A set of requirements shall be provided in the format requested by the supplier's designers.
- The Requirements Specification shall be approved by the client before any development work begins.
- Sufficient members of the client's organization will be available to participate in both the planning and execution of user acceptance testing.
- Change Requests shall be subject to a managed process of impact assessment before any development work is undertaken.

Deliverables

A full statement of the deliverables required must be provided; the more articulate, the better, since it represents a large proportion of what the client will get for their investment. The previous chapter identified a means by which to describe a deliverable, capturing its name, purpose, composition and quality criteria. For each relevant deliverable, this information should be sought. It is not easy, but if the risk of a failure to deliver is to be avoided, this is a sensible mitigation.

As above, the supplier may be equally interested that the client commits to a certain standard of productivity too. Therefore, certain key deliverables which the supplier requires from the client may also be defined and captured in the terms of reference. A good example would be the Requirements Specification, since both supplier and client will depend upon it to meet their own needs.

Timeline

A delivery date should be provided for each deliverable, allowing for both parties to plan their resources accordingly.

Dependencies

A clear understanding of the dependencies between deliverables, projects and teams is essential. The timeline above may capture some of this, identifying where one deliverable depends on another, but this section of the terms of reference may go further. It can pick out those specific hand-offs between the client and the supplier throughout the life of the project, and describe explicitly the nature of the dependence. Since these are the high-risk points where misunderstanding and delay can abound, many projects go further and create individual dependency agreements to ensure that the risks are managed.

Costs
The itemized cost of each resource may be included so that expectations are clear. For instance, the cost of the supplier's sales director's participation in the Project Steering Group might be waived whilst other supplier personnel, renowned for their specialist expertise, might be charged at a premium.

The charging model may be described fully, showing which elements are to be subject to which form of fee (eg time and materials, fixed, etc).

Skills, knowledge and experience
Where certain specific competencies are required, the client may wish to state their expectations. This will assist the supplier as they make provision for the resources who will be assigned to the project. The supplier too may wish for certain access to client expertise or authority.

Change control
The supplier has a crucial role to play in the management of changes. The change-control process must allow them to offer their expert, specialist opinion when considering an issue or Change Request. They must also be allowed to advise on the impact on costs and timescales, given that they may be a significant resource provider to the project. Therefore, the change-control process adopted by the project should be included in the terms of reference with specific attention drawn to the ways in which the supplier will be expected to participate.

Quality management
Since much of what the supplier will provide to the client will be in the form of deliverables, it is crucial that the terms of

reference make clear what quality control obligations are placed on each party. Whenever a deliverable is produced, it should progress through some form of quality control. As for change control (above), the supplier has a dual role to play. Firstly, their expertise in considering any deliverable's specialist quality criteria should be captured in the quality-control process. Secondly, it should be made clear that all deliverables produced by the supplier will be subject to a client-led quality assessment where the product is tested against its quality criteria to determine its fitness-for-purpose.

Delivery

Putting in place a shared governance for the project is only half the story. Once the terms of reference have been agreed, the client and supplier teams must act together to plan, build, test and deliver the project's deliverables.

Planning

Engage the supplier from the earliest point possible in the planning of the project. Their specialist insights will be of crucial importance. Furthermore, not only will they gain a clearer understanding of what is expected of them, they will also benefit from a fuller comprehension of the project's wider objectives. In this way, they may identify opportunities which the client would otherwise miss.

The lasting benefit of such early and integrated participation in planning is that the quality and reliability of estimates are inevitably improved. This results in a budget which is more likely to suit the needs of the project, and a better informed, more realistic, timescale.

Delegation

Having developed a deliverable-focused plan, it is important that those same deliverables are delegated by the Project Manager to members of the team. This is of particular importance where suppliers are concerned as it is yet another means by which they may be more effectively managed. In fact, the directive to produce a defined and agreed deliverable is only a part of the fuller instruction which is necessary if both parties are to completely understand their obligations. In the same way that the terms of reference describe the relationship between the two parties for the project, a 'Work Package' can serve to do the same for a single deliverable or a number of deliverables. So it is common when delegating to provide not only the description of the deliverable being commissioned, but also a supporting set of information, as follows:

- description of Work Package – the purpose of the work;
- plan – to show the context within which the work is to be undertaken;
- dependency diagram – to show the sequence of deliverables based on their dependence;
- deliverable descriptions – to describe the intended product;
- dependencies – to identify any further internal or external dependencies;
- prerequisite deliverables – to show which other deliverables will be needed in order for this work to commence;
- roles and responsibilities – to clarify the obligations that each party expect of each other;
- reporting arrangements – to explain when and how the parties will engage to understand progress and forecasts;
- skills/experience required – to make clear what competencies are needed to do the work;
- planned start/finish date – to state when, according to the plan, the work should start and end;
- planned effort/cost – to state what budget (expressed as person-day effort or monetary value) has been provisioned for the work;
- cost code – to represent the authority to undertake the work and allow it to be charged to a valid project code;
- escalation criteria – to set limits of authority for both parties;
- standards – to identify any techniques, processes or specific standards which are relevant to the work in question;
- other delivery criteria – to capture any other matters of importance, for example, the priority of the work in question.

Risk management

It is vital to benefit from the supplier's expertise and this is no more true than when identifying and mitigating risks. Given the vendor's supposed experience, it is likely that they will have encountered many of the risks which the present project may face, and will have considered the mitigations necessary to manage them. So, when conducting a review of the risks, invite your suppliers to participate. If they charge you for their time, consider it money well spent, for what you have bought is a greater assurance that together you can handle what the world may throw at you.

Change control

As described in the terms of reference above, the supplier has a crucial role to play in the continued management of change during the project's life. The diagram in Figure 8.2 was shown earlier in Chapter 6.

There are some very specific places during this process where a supplier may add great value. From the outset, they will be able to spot problems and the possible need for changes to be made.

FIGURE 8.2

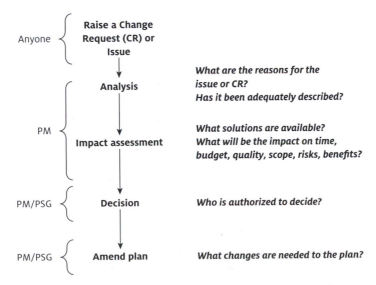

Although a cynical client's instinct may be to consider this as an opportunity to generate more work for the supplier, they have specific competence which a client would be unwise to ignore – and for which they are already paying.

During the analysis phase, the supplier's expertise can be used to better express the reasons for the Issue or Change Request. But their greatest contribution comes with the assessment of its impact. Since it may affect the timing, cost and quality of work (planned or already underway), the supplier's expertise must be one of a number of perspectives brought to bear on the challenge in question.

Finally, if the eventual decision is so significant as to warrant the Project Steering Group's intervention, the supplier's participation at that level as a Specialist authority will provide its other members with the authoritative opinion they may be unable to get from anywhere else.

Quality management

As mapped out in the terms of reference, the client and supplier each have obligations to produce deliverables which are fit for their intended purpose. This presents a further opportunity for the supplier's expertise to be used constructively and beneficially.

The diagram in Figure 8.3 illustrates the process of quality definition through development, testing and acceptance. The supplier has a role to play throughout. For deliverables which they themselves are to develop, they should be involved as the deliverable is first described, helping to define its quality criteria. Then, having built the deliverable they can present it to the client for its managed movement through quality control. Here, they must be available to answer questions and make fixes according to the terms agreed. It is by this process that the supplier delivers something which meets the client's expectations.

For deliverables which the client is to develop, the supplier role may be reversed. That is, they may be one of the parties to set quality expectations for what the client produces (as noted earlier, a Requirements Specification is a good example). When the deliverable is to be tested, it may well be the supplier who undertakes the test, providing the independence and expertise which is absent

FIGURE 8.3

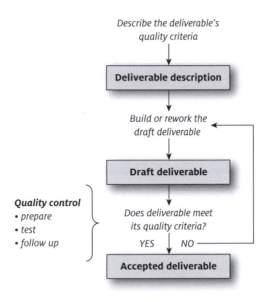

elsewhere in the project. And the deliverable's approval or acceptance may, in part, be provided by the supplier participating in the Project Steering Group.

Assurance

In the Case study, the procurement department appeared to have a part to play only when the damage had already been done. In practice, it is far better that the client–supplier relationship is assured throughout the project, rather than fixed (or discarded) at the end. So it is common practice to engage an independent body to understand and test the relationship, supplier services, deliverables and behaviours throughout the project. Think of it as a form of marriage guidance, commencing on the wedding day.

The client will clearly wish to ensure that the services and behaviours of their suppliers are to their desired standard. Thus, the independent assurer (someone from procurement, or perhaps another project) will regularly check the supplier's continued suitability across a range of measures, including:

- speed of delivery;
- speed of response;
- volume of delivery;
- quality of output;
- quality of resource;
- cost of output;
- efficiency of delivery.

The supplier can offer a similar assurance service through their participation in the Project Steering Group, offering guidance and advice in matters with which the client is unfamiliar. In this way, a more rewarding and fulfilling partnership can develop.

Which practices are to be avoided when engaging external suppliers?

In addition to those which are illegal or immoral, there are a few risky practices which should be avoided when subcontracting work to vendors.

Subcontracting risk

It would be nice to think that a problem might be swept from our desk and onto that of a specialist who might fix it. In truth, no project can be entirely delegated to another, for it is in the inherent nature of a project to require both client and supplier to engage, one building a solution for the other. At all times, the risk of failure ultimately remains with the client. If they choose to subcontract the whole project to a supplier, they themselves remain accountable for the risks, yet unable to control them. Those clients who fail to participate in their own projects should not be surprised when their suppliers are unable to meet their expectations.

Development versus testing

A common practice in computer systems development is to ensure that those who develop deliverables are not those who test them; to allow this to happen discourages the dispassionate, detached perspective needed to check a product's features. So those who write the code are seldom those who test it. It is a practice which can be transferred into projects, and was suggested in the quality management section above. Therefore, whilst suppliers should be expected to test their own work prior to submission, the client must ensure that the deliverable's approval as fit for purpose is theirs alone. The supplier can support the client in much the same way, testing and checking a client's deliverable prior to approval. An example of this would be where a supplier checks the robustness of a client-developed User Test Plan.

Quality versus cost

A common assumption amongst many organizations is that there are suppliers who can deliver things more cheaply than they can. Although this may be true, cost is only one feature which a project must manage. Time and quality are two other important features, and it is as true for projects as it is in any other walk of life: you get what you pay for. So when considering the advantages of a supplier's proposal, it is worth also ensuring that the project is structured in such a way as to gain greatest economic advantage, whilst managing the quality of what the project eventually produces. Therefore, many clients, especially those involved in computer systems development projects, will insist that the design of the solution is managed in-house by the client, not by the supplier. In this way, they retain responsibility for one of the most crucial phases of the project, whilst enjoying the benefit of the supplier's ability to build the solution at a cut price.

The tendency of many organizations over the last decade to subcontract work to parts of the world where costs are less has caused many of them to realize that what they are gaining in increased resource capacity they are losing in quality or cost. This is by no means to say that the ability of those developing systems in such parts of the world is poor, but rather that the complex movement of deliverables and instructions from one part of the world to another can have a negative impact on the eventual quality and/or cost.

The internal supplier

Everything described in this chapter may have been interpreted as referring only to external suppliers, but in fact, the solutions described apply as much to internal service providers as to those outside the business. The risks of failing to form effective working partnerships with supplier departments may be just as great for the project as failing to engage sufficiently well with an external party. A common consequence is that where one project is necessary, two arise; one allows for the specification of the client's needs, and the next delivers the solution. The unnecessary gap created between them serves only to present a barrier over which needs and solutions are awkwardly negotiated. Far better that client and supplier respect the needs of the project to accommodate them both in its successful management.

Conclusion

A project is a vehicle which allows for the various parties to achieve their expectations. However, those expectations may often be divergent and antagonistic. Yet, as some impossible marriages seem to survive, success has much to do with a mutual understanding and respect for each other's aspirations, different as they may be. In a project, it is truly to the benefit of all that 'opposites attract'.

SUMMARY

- Invite a senior member (or members) of your supplier to participate in the Project Steering Group such that they have a vested interest in its success.
- Require the sponsor to own the commercial relationship with your suppliers so that the risks to the project's viability are managed.
- Choose charging models which are suited to the supplier's strengths, and to the deliverables or services being purchased.
- Mix and match charging models according to the variety of products and services being purchased.
- Do not assume that a contract with a supplier to deliver operational services will be suited to the needs of a unique project.
- Develop terms of reference together that meet the unique needs of the project, and reflect both the shared and divergent ambitions of client and supplier.
- Ensure that the terms of reference become known as a component of the contract between the parties.
- Take advantage of the supplier's expertise, not merely their resource capacity.
- Delegate clear, agreed deliverables to the supplier, within a realistically considered Work Package.
- Practise mutual assurance: assure yourself of the supplier's continued suitability, and give them the opportunity to alert you to your own weaknesses.
- Don't imagine that you can subcontract the entire risk of a project to a supplier: as the client, the risk remains with you, and the project is your vehicle to mitigate it.
- Treat internal service providers as you would external suppliers.

CHAPTER NINE

TAKE CORRECTIVE ACTION; DON'T JUST WRITE ABOUT IT

This chapter covers:

- the relationship and difference between project reporting and project control;
- the importance of tailoring reports to suit the audiences required to act on them;
- the way in which the management of project information can dictate behaviour.

Whenever an important or controversial project begins, a flood of people will take an interest in it. 'Keep me informed,' they say, as if by so doing, the likelihood of its failure might be lessened. And as more people take an interest, their information demands become weightier and more complex, placing an ever greater burden on the Project Manager to satisfy their needs. What often follows is a recognition that a separated reporting function is needed to handle the capture of project data and its transformation into communicable information. Yet, in spite of all of these reports, and the tiers of interested parties who ask to receive them, and the ranks of officers charged with producing them, costs increase, deadlines are delayed or missed, quality expectations are unsatisfied and, occasionally, the very benefits required from the endeavour do not materialize. So it is a fallacy to believe that:

> *Myth 9: By reporting progress, we're controlling it.*

This chapter will focus on the importance and practice of separating project reporting from project control.

CASE STUDY

Two international organizations announced their intention to merge, citing the benefits of being able to offer the market a wider range of combined products and services, and the potential to reduce their overall cost of operation. An integration programme was conceived to achieve a swift amalgamation of the two businesses.

Given the pressure placed upon him to achieve the demanding objectives, the programme director created a 'command and control' organization structure that would allow him to quickly pass instructions to the pyramid beneath, and receive information in return. This organization structure was formed around a central hierarchy of 'Programme offices', each one corresponding with the tiers of management beneath the programme director. These Programme offices would be responsible for the efficient movement of information up and down the programme organization, and ensure that a consistent approach to management was ensured.

To begin with, the logical structure was appreciated for its simplicity. Where any problem existed that could not be solved locally, the escalation route through the Programme offices was straightforward. In particular, participants were grateful for the willingness of the programme director to so readily accept such a pivotal and personal responsibility for delivering the change.

As the months passed, the unbelievable complexity of the programme became clear. The logistics and dependencies were challenging enough, but the need to maintain and grow the business in parallel to its transformation added an acute commercial risk. Since the market and stock value were highly sensitive to the progress of the transformation, clear deadlines, budgets and savings had to be identified. In part, this is what the programme director delegated through the reporting structure beneath him.

However, as the various managers involved throughout the programme encountered challenges which they could not overcome, they recorded them with the support of their local Programme office and awaited a response. Since no one in the Programme office had the slightest idea how to solve the challenges, they passed them upwards through the tiers above until they eventually landed on the programme director's desk. Pretty soon, the programme director was inundated with tactical problems he could not piece together, and was therefore unable to manage the programme at a strategic level, which was his priority. He was swamped with data, but needed *information*.

This was similar to the challenge being faced by others in the organization. Everyone needed information in order to understand the programme. As the Programme offices compiled reports showing what progress had been achieved and what challenges the organization faced, there was a hungry band of managers throughout the business demanding more. So the role of the Programme offices became ever more important as the demands for management information increased.

As they received information demands from the Programme offices, the Project Managers each turned to their own unique data source: their individual project plans. But since the programme director required information which was consistent across all of the projects within the programme, the Programme offices realized they would have to insist upon a very specific and consistent format for project plans. They issued an instruction mandating that not only must all project plans conform to a certain standard, but they must also contain certain identical milestones.

The Project Managers might have been persuaded of the need to amend their plans to comply with the common format, but for many of them, the inclusion of the standard milestones made little sense since their projects were each unique. What exacerbated the dilemma further was the Programme offices' increasing intransigence; they were making demands of Project Managers, yet without any real understanding of the nature of their projects, nor of the competencies needed to manage them. Having been instructed to rewrite their project plans to accommodate the 40 or so 'minimum milestones' mandated by the Programme office, several Project Managers wondered what value was to be had from such significant rework.

As some Project Managers either rebelled or found the minimum milestones to be nonsensical for their projects, the Programme offices put in place a set of Key Performance Indicators (KPIs) which sought to measure the health of each project. In this way, they intended to identify projects which were non-conformant. The KPIs were rolled out across the programme. People from the Programme offices sought time in the Project Managers' diaries to make performance measurements against a range of mandated standards. These interventions were referred to as Project health checks. The information was collated and passed upwards through the tiers, then onwards to the programme director.

Knowing that they were being judged on the format of their plans, the frequency of their reports and their inclusion of predefined minimum milestones, the Project Managers adapted their behaviours and did as they were instructed.

Within six months, the programme was discovered to be wading in a sea of self-perpetuating bureaucracy. The multitude of reports failed to describe the real programme. The KPIs were found to have resulted in the desired standardization of plans and reports, but had eliminated the unique content which lay at the heart of each project. Project Managers and their sponsors had been rendered powerless, submitting to the authority of the Programme office hierarchy. And the Programme offices were found to be filled with a majority of staff who, whilst excellent and efficient administrators, had never managed a project themselves.

The programme director was dismissed and replaced. Despite the reporting edifice that had been created, there remained a small minority who were both sufficiently empowered and competent to take corrective decisions. Under a new leadership, these qualities were given greater prominence, and grew as a result. The priority of KPIs which drove standardization and reporting compliance was lessened in favour of those which promoted delivery and control.

What this means

Project and Programme offices should work within their terms of reference

Project and Programme offices serve a crucial and invaluable service. Theirs may be a complex brief with high stakeholder expectations. Yet, without a clear and explicit set of responsibilities, the role is one which can rapidly exceed its brief, or fail to add sufficient value. In the Case study, the Programme offices assumed responsibilities for which they had neither the competence nor authority. This was because the programme director confused the reporting hierarchy for the tiers of management which would ultimately be held accountable for success or failure. In allowing such authority to grow within the Programme offices, the centre of power needed to control progress was tilted away from those who had the competence to do so.

'Consistency of management' is the wrong target

As the Programme offices' focus on reporting became ever more important, their attention focused on obtaining data in a consistent format. They took this to mean that projects had to be managed in a uniform way. Although the actions they took consequently improved standardization, they failed to account for the quality of management needed to govern such a wide range of unique and individually challenged projects. Therefore, the talents of Project Managers and sponsors to adapt their management to the level of project risk were favoured less than the importance of a consistent approach. As a result, the condition in which the programme was left for the incoming programme director was consistent, but consistently poor.

You get the behaviours you reward

The programme had been moulded around what the Programme offices believed were desirable values. These included the production of plans in a common format, the standard of project reports and the timeliness of data submissions. That these behaviours were given such weight was problem enough as it discouraged Project Managers and sponsors from pursuing their own targets. But it was compounded by the introduction of KPIs which served to reward and penalize a limited set of behaviours. The programme was transformed from one which contained a range of talents making varied contributions to a homogeny of people reporting an ever-worsening scenario.

The consequences of ignoring the imperative

When an organization structure becomes too focused on the gathering, formatting and consideration of management information, there can be little time or interest left over for the control of projects. In turn, the culture progressively adapts to become intelligence obsessed rather than action focused. In this way, an organization loses its competence to fix problems, preferring instead to distribute reports rather than delegate control. Information should be gathered for the sole purpose of taking corrective action, rather than as an end in itself.

The longer-term consequences manifest themselves in the form of bureaucracies which can add little value. Project and

Programme offices are transformed from bodies which can genuinely support and assure the initiatives to those which simply add cost, not value.

Institutions – not just the individual projects within them – become progressively more interested in the costly pursuit of consistency than in creative, intuitive and effective control.

The solutions

'Reporting' and 'control' are closely associated. Their relationship may be better understood with reference to the 'control cycle', illustrated in Figure 9.1.

Whoever has planned and delegated the work may also be responsible for monitoring progress, and capturing what they have learned in reports of various kinds. However, for the project to remain on target requires that any variances are acted upon. It is this corrective action which is what is meant by 'control'. On taking the necessary steps to bring things back on course, the plan may be amended to reflect changes, and the cycle begins again.

Many report writers will pride themselves on their ability to describe clearly the project's status. So they will state what budget

FIGURE 9.1

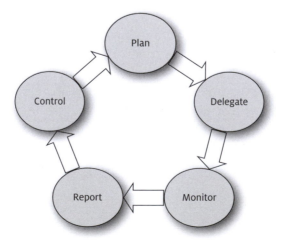

has been consumed, what has been delivered, what problems exist and so forth. Yet this information gives us little if anything upon which to act. Knowing where we are is unhelpful; rather, any project, portfolio or programme report must be able to forecast its likely status upon completion. Failure to do this suggests that the person in charge of the change, be they a project or programme manager, has not been replanning as the initiative has progressed, and that all they are presently able to record is what has happened to date. Such information tells us nothing about where the actions will be needed to steer the endeavour to a successful close.

Therefore, in any project, portfolio or programme report, it is crucial to know not merely what the project has achieved to date, but in what condition it is expected to be at the point of closure. It is for this reason that I personally prefer the title Project Forecast Report to Project Status Report.

Build effective reports

Select an appropriate frequency of production

How frequently any project steps through the control cycle must take account of:

- the manager's personal aversion to risk;
- the urgency and importance of the work;
- the volume of work to be undertaken;
- the present position in the project life cycle;
- the expertise of the people doing the work.

Therefore, if a report of a project's progress is to be produced every month, it follows that variances may only be identified – and corrected – every month. For some projects, this may be three weeks too late. So, subject to a maximum frequency of a month, each project should be given the opportunity to choose their own frequency of reporting, and not have a standard imposed on them which is unsuited to its unique features.

Measure and report the things you really need to control

The reporting and the creation of information from data can quickly become an industry. If the information is to be useful, it should serve to identify where control must be exercised. So it follows that one should measure and report the things one wishes to control.

In the Case study, KPIs were created to identify the extent to which performance targets were being met. For example, they sought to know which projects were delivering their Forecast Reports on time, and thus created a KPI which would enable them to measure it. In this way, they not only gained the information they needed in order to take the actions they felt necessary, but they also changed the behaviours of Project Managers as a result. What they failed to consider was that, although effective, the KPIs caused a change in behaviours which delivered little value to the business. So although they were measuring and reporting effectively, they had failed to pick a set of really important measures.

> Wrongly, many organizations decide what to measure before they've chosen what it is they need to control.

The creation of KPIs – and the bureaucracy which sits behind them – should begin with the most senior members of the organization deciding what objectives it must meet. When they have done so, they can decide what indicators will suggest the extent to which those objectives are being met. Furthermore, those objectives may be shared with those in the tier of management below so that they may create some complementary targets and performance measures of their own. And so the objectives are progressively decomposed throughout the organization, ensuring everyone's behaviours are consistent in achieving the targets to which they are all contributing.

Figure 9.2 presents an illustration.

FIGURE 9.2

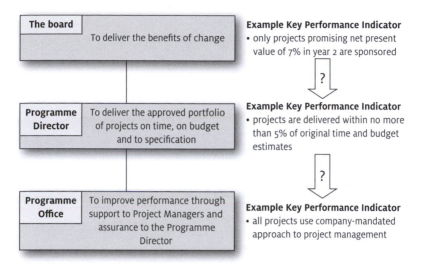

Taking the Case study as inspiration, three levels of a management hierarchy are shown, each with a single example objective and corresponding Key Performance Indicator. When measured, these will suggest the extent to which that management team is achieving the objective they have been set. They should also allow for the management level beneath to understand what matters to their superiors. Yet in the example given, it may be seen how each level of management has set objectives for itself which make little if any contribution to those above. For example, the Programme office has a performance objective for which the Key Performance Indicator is not only unsuitable, but encourages a behaviour which will deliver consistency, not the time, cost and quality targets desired by the programme director, nor the benefit expectations set by the board.

Therefore, each level of management should have a set of measurable objectives which are consistent with the organization's aspirations. For those key bodies engaged in the management of change, these may appear as follows:

The Change Management Team

The Change Management Team's objective is:

- To identify, prioritize, commission and deliver a balanced, value-rich mix of projects within a budget, aligned to the business's change objectives.

Its Key Performance Indicators may be:

- All participants carry the authority needed to make any decision required of them.
- Participants have been drawn from all areas from which decisions are needed.
- Participants remain committed to their responsibilities for the course of the CMT's operation.
- The mix of projects contributes to the achievement of defined business objectives as planned.
- Commercial and strategic targets are met.
- Projects within the portfolio are being delivered on time and on budget.
- Projects are producing results of acceptable quality.
- Resources across the portfolio are being efficiently administered.
- Change is being actively balanced against the need to deliver BAU.

Project Steering Group

The Project Steering Group's objective is:

- To deliver the expectations described in the Business Case.

Its Key Performance Indicators may be:

- The Business Case is maintained, is always accessible, and illustrates the difference between the company's total effort or investment in the project compared with the income or benefit from it.

- The project produces a value-adding outcome as identified in the Business Case.
- The group has identified and empowered a single Project Manager to plan, coordinate and control the project.
- The group has been able to set and apply escalation conditions for the Project Manager.
- The group has applied 'management by exception', where the group is immediately informed by the Project Manager if forecast timings and costs are outside agreed escalation conditions.
- The group has been able to provide sufficient resources of the necessary quality to allow the plan to be fulfilled.

Project Manager

The Project Manager's objective is:

- To deliver the project's deliverables in accordance with the most recently authorized expectations of timescale, cost and quality.

The Project Manager's Key Performance Indicators may be:

- There is an authorized plan that shows progress to date and forecasts for time, cost and quality.
- All plans clearly identify the deliverables to be produced.
- Escalation conditions for time and cost have been agreed with the Project Steering Group and are being applied.
- There is a record demonstrating that any changes to scope, timescale, cost and benefits have been approved by those who have authority to do so.
- There is a record of risks to the project, together with mitigation plans and actions.
- The Project Steering Group is being kept regularly and sufficiently informed through progress/forecast reports.
- The most recently authorized expectations of time, cost and quality have been met.

Gather the data needed to measure the objective

If a set of objectives as outlined above are to be met, certain crucial data must be gathered in order that a full and true picture may be communicated and acted upon. The Key Performance Indicators listed above suggest the need for a considerable quantity of data. For instance, if a Project Manager's success is truly to be judged in part on their keeping 'a record demonstrating that any changes to scope, timescale, cost and benefits have been approved by those who have authority to do so', evidence of that record, and its efficacy, must be sought.

To keep data and information management to a reasonable and practical level, there are certain reports which will be of particular value. In order to create these (examples of which will appear at the end of this section), some essential data must be captured in a very particular format, as follows:

An authorized baseline

In Chapter 6, a baseline was described as follows:

> A baseline is an authorized record of a project variable at a specific point in time. Amongst others, a baseline may be set for the project's timescale, budget, scope or benefits. Setting a baseline is like taking a date-stamped photograph of the project. It shows what the project looked like at a point in time – what it was expected to cost, when it was due to deliver, what it would produce, what value it would confer on the organization, and so forth. A great benefit of a baseline is to allow for the consequence of a change to be assessed in order that a decision can be made to accept it or not. Without a baseline, it becomes impossible to know what impact a change may have on any of the project's variables, resulting in either a reluctance to accept any change at all, or the accommodation of changes without knowledge of the consequence.
>
> One of the reasons why Project Managers place such great importance on obtaining approval of the Project Plan and Business Case at the outset is because the Project Steering Group's acceptance of them transforms the documents into the baseline against which success will be measured. Whenever a request to change the project

is encountered, for whatever reason and from whomsoever it may originate, an assessment may be carried out to understand its impact on the Project Plan and Business Case. If any of the baseline measures look to be impacted in any serious way, the Project Manager may seek the Project Steering Group's approval to have them changed, or 're-baselined'.

A clearly identified 'forecast'

With a baseline in place, it is necessary to know what progress has been made to date, and to what extent such progress suggests a successful meeting of the relevant target.

For date-based information, people working on the production of deliverables are asked when they are now forecast to complete, given that much may have changed since the plan was baselined.

For financial or numeric information, it is necessary to know what has actually been spent or achieved to date (known as the 'Actual to date'), and what remains to be spent or achieved by the end of the project (known as the 'Estimate to complete'). When these two figures are added together, it is possible to calculate a new 'Forecast at completion' which, when compared to the baseline, establishes the variation.

Identified variation

Without a clear statement of the variance between the baseline and the revised forecast, it becomes difficult to know if any problems exist, where they are, how extreme or damaging they may be, and who should be charged with taking corrective action to fix them. So any report which fails to identify the variance between the baseline and the forecast is seriously failing in its purpose.

Extent of variation

The concept and practice of 'escalation conditions' were described in Chapter 3, and are repeated here:

The Project Steering Group provides its Project Manager with a degree of time and budgetary flexibility so that the manager may act on their own authority within pre-agreed constraints. So if the escalation conditions for time and cost have been set for ±two weeks and ±5 per cent respectively, the Project Steering Group need not be involved in or troubled by the daily management of the project as long as its forecast end date does not vary by more or less than two weeks and the forecast cost remains within ±5 per cent of its target. If at any time the Project Manager forecasts that the project will not be completed within the agreed escalation conditions, the problem must be escalated immediately to the Project Steering Group for a decision on how to proceed as the Project Manager's boundaries of authority have been breached. Crucially, escalation conditions do not mean that the Project Steering Group is allowing their Project Manager to overspend or deliver late. The conditions provide the flexibility which the Project Manager will need to allow their daily management of the project to continue unhindered, whilst underlining the Project Steering Group's power to act if the project should be forecast to veer too far off track.

It is this practice which can be applied to variations identified in reports, such that an action owner may be identified and held to account.

Implement some simple project reports

Once such data is maintained, it becomes a relatively straight-forward matter to draw it together into a series of management information reports which suit the various audiences to whom they are addressed, and on whom accountability is placed for any corrective action needed.

The hierarchy of reports matches the hierarchy of management. Figure 9.3 shows an example report which might suit a Project Manager.

For Project Steering Groups, whose success is measured in terms of the extent to which the benefits outweigh the costs, a different form or report is required which might look like Figure 9.4.

This shows how ticket sales (which were a measure of the quality output from the project) are forecast to have a direct impact on the Business Case.

The management information suited to the Change Management Team might look something like Figure 9.5.

FIGURE 9.3

Time management

	Baseline	Actual or forecast end date	Variance	Reason	Condition (red / amber / green)	Action/responsibility
Milestone 1	10/08	15/08	−5		Red	
Milestone 3	17/09	19/09	−2		Amber	
Milestone 6	14/10	15/10	−1		Amber	
Project closure	**11/11**	**11/11**	**0**		**Green**	

Cost management

	Baseline A	Actual to date B	Estimate to complete C	Forecast at completion D (B+C)	Variance E (D−A)	Reason	Condition (red / amber / green)	Action/ responsibility
Resource 1	10,000	7,000	5,000	12,000	2,000		Amber	
Resource 2	8,000	3,000	3,000	6,000	−2,000		Amber	
Resource 3	5,000	0	5,000	5,000	0		Green	
Total	**23,000**	**10,000**	**13,000**	**23,000**	**0**		**Green**	

Quality management

	Baseline A	Actual to date B	Estimate to complete C	Forecast at completion D (B+C)	Variance E (D−A)	Reason	Condition (red / amber / green)	Action/ responsibility
eg tickets sold	1,500	40	900	940	−560		Red	

FIGURE 9.4

Time management

	Baseline	Actual or forecast end date	Variance	Reason	Condition (red / amber / green)	Action/ responsibility
Project closure	11/11	11/11	0		Green	

Cost management

	Baseline A	Actual to date B	Estimate to complete C	Forecast at completion D (B+C)	Variance E (D−A)	Reason	Condition (red / amber / green)	Action/ responsibility
TOTAL	23,000	10,000	13,000	23,000	0		Green	

Quality management

	Baseline A	Actual to date B	Estimate to complete C	Forecast at completion D (B+C)	Variance E (D−A)	Reason	Condition (red / amber / green)	Action/ responsibility
eg ticket sales	1,500	40	900	940	−560		Red	

Business Case management

	Baseline A	Actual to date B	Estimate to complete C	Forecast at completion D (B+C)	Variance E (D−A)	Reason	Condition (red / amber / green)	Action/ responsibility
Benefits eg ticket sales	90,000	2,400	54,000	56,400	−33,600		Red	
Costs	23,000	10,000	13,000	23,000	0		Green	
Net	67,000	−7,600	41,000	33,400	−33,600		Red	

FIGURE 9.5

		Project One	Project Two	Project Three
BACKGROUND	**ID**	1	2	3
	Last Health check Date	12-Jan	22-Jun	22-Jun
	Health-checker	Pete Robbins	Maggie Jones	Henry Jenson
	Project Start Date	10-Dec	10-Sep	01-Aug
PSG	**Sponsor**	Brad Somerville	Mark Knowles	Matthew Mossop
	User Authority	Kevin Quinn	Helen Smith	Ruby Roberts
	Specialist Authority	Mark Johnson	Bupinda Patel	James Skimming
PM	**Project Manager**	Will Stevens	Harry King	Harry King
TIME	**Baseline End Date**	31-May	10-Jun	11-Nov
	Forecast End Date	31-May	30-Sep	11-Nov
	Variance (weeks)	*0*	*−16*	*0*
	Escalation Conditions (weeks)	*2*	*2*	*1*
	Within Escalation Conditions?	*Yes*	*No*	*Yes*
COST	**Baseline Budget ($)**	2,026,971	101,923	23,000
	Forecast Budget ($)	2,026,971	115,000	23,000
	Variance ($)	*0*	*−13,077*	*0*
	Escalation Conditions %	*10*	*10*	*10*
	Within Escalation Conditions?	*Yes*	*No*	*No*
BENEFITS	**Baseline Benefits ($)**	2,703,836	200,101	90,000
	Forecast Benefits ($)	2,703,836	200,101	56,400
	Variance ($)	*0*	*0*	*−33,600*
	Escalation Conditions %	*10*	*10*	*10*
	Within Escalation Conditions?	*Yes*	*Yes*	*No*
BUSINESS CASE	**Baseline Net ($)**	676,865	98,178	67,000
	Forecast Net ($)	676,865	85,101	33,400
	Variance ($)	*0*	*−13,077*	*−33,600*
	Escalation Conditions %	*10*	*10*	*10*
	Within Escalation Conditions?	*Yes*	*No*	*No*

This body has information which illustrates the relative status and forecast for each of the various projects within their remit, allowing them to pick on those which have exceeded their escalation conditions and which therefore require their intervention and authority. A further report which might assist in their work will be an updated version of Figure 2.7, described earlier in Chapter 2.

Empower the right people

In the Case study, the programme director allowed the hierarchy of Programme offices to be responsible for not only gathering and reporting information, but for taking corrective action too. This latter responsibility was completely unsuited to their competencies and authority. They exceeded their remit, and went further by imposing too many additional activities on an already challenged management team.

It is quite acceptable, and usual, for a Project or Programme office to take away some of the monitoring and reporting burden from Project Managers and other change managers. But those who are held accountable for planning and delivering the project and the change must also be charged with controlling progress.

Here are terms of reference for a Project or Programme office, taking account of the many ways in which it may be designed and implemented.

Role purpose:

- to assist the Project Manager and project team;
- to assure the Project Steering Group that the project management environment is, and continues to be, fit for its intended purpose;
- to assist and assure the Change Management Team in their governance of the portfolio.

Benefits of role:

- better use of scarce skills;
- development arena for project management expertise;

- faster and more accurate impact assessment of changes and risks;
- application of common standards;
- stronger application of a common management discipline;
- central and single repository for management information;
- flexible service provision according to need;
- greater confidence in alignment of projects to strategic imperatives.

Responsibilities (*the responsibilities which follow have been divided into sections to take account of the variety of ways in which the Programme or Project office may have been implemented*):

to support and/or assure the Change Management Team:

- contribute to the development and continued management of the portfolio plan;
- develop and maintain the organization's systemized approach to project management;
- monitor progress of all projects against the portfolio plan, prepare portfolio forecast reports and alert Change Management Team to variances;
- assure the integrity of products being delivered by the portfolio, particularly regarding:
  - scope, to confirm that duplication or omissions are minimized;
  - value, to provide assurance that projects are delivering to cost with a clear focus on benefits management;
  - competencies, to ensure that the organization's skills are being applied effectively and efficiently;
  - timescale, to determine that projects remain focused on time targets and that dependencies are being honoured;
  - strategic fit, to assure the project management team that projects have been prioritized to meet the organization's strategic imperatives;
  - compliance, to demonstrate that standards and procedures are being respected.
- conduct health checks and propose solutions;
- assess and advise on the implications of changes to the portfolio plan;

- provide support in using tools or techniques for managing the portfolio or projects;
- identify and satisfy training needs;
- develop and maintain a register of the organization's project resources and skills;
- facilitate portfolio co-ordination and communication sessions;
- track and measure the realization of benefits from projects.

to support and/or assure the Project Steering Group:

- help to link projects to the organization's strategic imperatives;
- advise on initiation procedures;
- advise on identifying and managing benefits in the Business Case;
- help the sponsor to maintain the Business Case;
- help to prepare Project Steering Group meetings;
- propose and/or conduct project health checks;
- advise on closure procedures;
- support the sponsor during the benefits realization stage.

to support the Project Manager with:

- planning:
  - help the Project Manager to prepare the project plan;
  - facilitate and/or administer planning sessions;
  - assist in developing estimates;
  - help the Project Manager prepare changes to plans where escalation conditions have been breached;
  - propose recovery actions where escalation conditions have been breached.
- monitoring and reporting:
  - make sure that time recording and forecast reporting procedures are being applied;
  - produce the Project Forecast Report for the Project Manager, alerting him to key variances;
  - administer change control procedures;
  - assess the effect of Change Requests and Issues;
  - facilitate the regular identification of risks;

- maintain and update the Business Case, particularly regarding costs;
  - make sure that all quality controls are applied through maintaining the product quality log;
  - attend quality reviews when appropriate to make sure they are adequate;
  - assist in closing the project.
- administration:
  - coordinate all quality control activities;
  - check or complete timesheet information on behalf of all project resources;
  - minute all project meetings;
  - administer the project's configuration management;
  - identify training requirements and assist in their resolution;
  - gather improvements to the systemized approach to project management.
- consultancy:
  - coach project personnel in project management;
  - provide project planning support and assistance to all project personnel;
  - provide guidance on assorted specialist matters;
  - develop and/or support automated tools or techniques;
  - provide support to improve the accuracy of estimates.

Measures of success:

- The Programme or Project office addresses the issues and opportunities it was put in place to overcome.
- The costs of its implementation and operation are outweighed by the benefits it delivers.
- The selected products and services have been prioritized to make sure the benefits are realized swiftly.
- Its position in the organization is clear.
- It is offering more than an administrative service.
- The audience(s) it serves is satisfied with the products and services it is providing.

Adapt the culture

There are several things which may be done to ensure that reports do not become an end in themselves, and that the all-important corrective actions are taken by the right people.

Remove blockers

There are some common arguments used by some people in favour of not creating reports.

There are too many to produce

With so many stakeholders taking an interest in the project, it is not unusual for information demands to be high. If these are legitimate, then it may be possible to consider the use of a Project or Programme office to take away some of the reporting burden from the Project Manager. If some of the information requests are considered unnecessary or not of sufficient importance, the Project Steering Group can use their authority to lessen or remove any unauthorized demands on their Project Manager's time. Alternatively, a charge may be made for the report, passing on its cost of production to the party who requested it.

An option which is increasing in popularity is to populate and maintain a database with the data illustrated in Figures 9.3, 9.4 and 9.5, and allow others to interrogate it for themselves, drawing off whatever reports they wish.

They take too much time and effort to compile

There are several reasons why this may be cited as an argument:

- The reporting demands are over-complex – keep the reporting format as simple as possible, wording to a minimum and actions clear. The example in Figures 9.3, 9.4 and 9.5 may serve as a place from which to begin. Indeed, it may be possible to adopt a format for the plan which is almost identical to those illustrated in Figures 9.3, 9.4 and 9.5. In this way, the plan *becomes* the report – anyone wishing to know what is the present forecast may scrutinize the plan and understand what actions are in place to address any variances.

- Key management documents (such as the project plan) have not been sufficiently maintained with progress data – this is highly undesirable. If a project manager has allowed this to happen without good reason, they may need to be supported in their role by a coach, offered training, or removed from their role.
- Gathering progress data is too complex – this may be the case if the people involved in the project are geographically separated, or if there are a great number of suppliers involved. In either case, a systemized approach may be needed, including the use of time-sheets to formally record the time committed by the team.

Encourage action

Whenever a forecast report has been produced, require the person who developed it to present it to the relevant managers. In this way, actions and solutions for problems identified in the report become the focus, not the report itself.

It may also be advantageous to have a great number of projects present their reports at the same time, perhaps in a form of 'Star Chamber'. Not only does this allow for the opportunity to challenge, but also creates something of a supportive and competitive spirit amongst Project Managers.

Aside from any very tailored actions which may be identified to overcome a specific challenge, the alternatives open to those who manage change are reasonably limited. In Chapter 6, where change control was considered, the following options were identified:

- *to maintain control while keeping to a fixed deadline:*
  - *more resources may be necessary;*
  - *faster resources may be needed;*
  - *quality and/or quality checks may have to be reduced;*
  - *the scope of what is delivered may have to be reduced;*
  - *overtime/weekend work may have to be increased;*
  - *holidays may have to be cancelled.*
- *to maintain control while working within a fixed budget:*
  - *cheaper resources may be required;*
  - *fewer resources may be employed;*
  - *quality and/or quality checks may have to be reduced;*

- *the scope of what is delivered may have to be reduced;*
- *delivery dates may have to be delayed;*
- *overtime/weekend work may have to be reduced;*
- *holidays may have to be cancelled.*

- *to maintain control while meeting the original quality and content expectations:*
  - *more resources may be necessary;*
  - *'better' resources may be needed;*
  - *quality processes, including tests, may have to be improved;*
  - *customer expectations may have to be better managed;*
  - *delivery dates may have to be delayed;*
  - *discounts may have to be offered;*
  - *some components may have to be deferred until later.*

Other, stark options include:

- *delivering late;*
- *delivering over budget;*
- *delivering lower quality or reduced scope;*
- *if the Business Case is compromised, cancelling the project.*

Lead by example

If an action needs the engagement of someone in a position of senior authority, it is to be advised that they acknowledge their obligation, and do what they can to deliver an answer. If they fail in this responsibility, the project will suffer for want of a solution, and faith will have been lost in the commitment of senior managers.

Conclusion

When a project is underway, one of the most common management errors is to consider its present state in preference to its forecast condition at the point of completion. So, many managers live in hope that their project will complete somewhere in the region of their expectations despite having no supporting evidence. That they do this may be because the regular gathering, formatting and reforecasting of project data is, frankly, hard work. But planning does not stop when the project begins. It is a continuous activity which allows for work to be reassessed in light of changes, intended or otherwise.

The reports we produce must bring to life what has changed since we first planned the project, and direct the right people to take the corrective action that these expensive, risky endeavours deserve.

SUMMARY

- Like everyone else, a Project or Programme office must work within the confines of terms of reference.
- The cost of designing and delivering management reports is one which must be off set by the benefits of the control they encourage.
- Management reports should be tailored to the control needs of their audience.
- A specific set of essential data is necessary if all levels in the management hierarchy are to get what they need.
- Blockers which inhibit those who gather and create essential management information should be removed.
- A report which describes the present status of a project is much less useful than one which describes its potential condition on completion.
- 'Variance' is the most important piece of management information available as it determines whether corrective action is required, and to whom that action falls.
- Those who receive and read reports must be empowered to act on the information they receive.

CHAPTER TEN

IDENTIFY AND MITIGATE RISKS BEFORE IT IS TOO LATE

This chapter covers:

- the use of risk management as a tool to justify change;
- the consideration of risk management as a state of mind, rather than as a process;
- the role of risk management during the conception, initiation and delivery of change.

On entering an organization for the first time, or when attempting to understand a project or programme of change, it is always helpful to ask a single, searching question: what are the risks? In doing so, people's underlying worries and concerns are lifted from out of their subconscious and into the light where they may be faced and managed. Yet a great many organizations, either willingly or out of ignorance, seek to avoid facing risks. They choose to manage problems once they have been realized, as if this makes them easier to tackle. It may be true that a problem well described is a problem half-solved, but it is possible to describe and manage a problem before it has happened. Effective risk management helps us to save money, time and further exposure by identifying, examining and mitigating potential problems before they materialize. So although some people may consider it overly pessimistic to dwell on what might go wrong, a risk-centric attitude prepares individuals and organizations to better avoid trouble, or to respond more effectively when it arrives.

So it is not always more effective to believe that:

> *Myth 10: We'll deal best with problems as they arise.*

This chapter will consider the ways in which the management of projects and the management of risk are entwined.

CASE STUDY

Over the years, an organization had developed an enormous and complex 'data warehouse' which housed its store of customer data. When used efficiently, the data warehouse offered the potential to provide insights into customer behaviours, trends and needs which might otherwise have gone unnoticed. This enabled the organization to beat their competitors to market with new products and services. It was a phenomenal and crucial asset of the business.

The volume of the data it housed grew daily, and the demands being made of it placed the computer processor under ever greater pressure. Yet the business was relentless in its use of the data warehouse, depending on it to provide a continued market advantage. The storage capacity and processor had both been upgraded several times to allow for growth. The supplier who provided the hardware on which the data warehouse was founded had temporarily provided free access to an additional processor. This had partially mitigated further performance issues. However, the period during which the business had free use of the processor was drawing to a close. Before very long, low capacity and poor speed would be more than a passing annoyance, becoming business-critical issues. The data warehouse had become a victim of its own success. It seemed that another investment would be needed to upgrade the warehouse yet again.

A Business Case was constructed, outlining the present limitations and describing how an investment in increased processor speed and disc capacity would allow for further revenues to be generated from yet more intelligence about customers.

The head of IT was presented with the Business Case. He carefully considered the forecast revenues which, it was argued, would come from the considerable investment his own department would have to make in further hardware. He was not convinced. He sent it spinning back across the desk at its hapless author. 'We've only just upsized the processor and drives and already they're approaching full capacity! Tell your bosses I'm not going to sign another cheque until we can find an alternative to buying more and more hardware.' As if to cement his point, he added that he would also be resisting pressure to pay for the supplier's extra processor capacity when it became chargeable in a few months' time.

The business was in uproar! Who was this person to place such a constraint on the organization's growth? IT was a service provider and should do as it was told! Yet the head of IT stuck to his position and produced some evidence which showed how inefficiently the data warehouse was being used. Database queries and reports were being written by people with little data management experience, resulting in jobs which ran for hours and at peak times during the day. None of the jobs was prioritized, so a relatively trivial database enquiry might prevent a crucial one from running. And whilst plenty of people tinkered with its structure and content there was no one to oversee the use of the data warehouse as a business asset.

So the business and IT developed a joint Business Case to mitigate the risks of doing nothing. In articulating them, an entirely different picture emerged within which an alternative set of challenges led to a different solution.

In considering the risks of doing nothing rather than the opportunity for revenue growth, a range of blockers was uncovered:

- The absence of any strategic management of the data warehouse was resulting in its poor and inefficient structure and development.

- The absence of any prioritization of demand made on the data warehouse was leading to the delay of essential queries and reports, and the creation of workload peaks for which the processor was insufficiently powerful.
- The growth of the supporting hardware had become unpredictable, leading to erratic budgetary demands.
- The growth in user demand, although causing the IT infrastructure to become unstable, could not (and should not) be curtailed as the asset was considered to belong to the business and would ultimately lead to revenue growth.
- The data held in the data warehouse was poorly structured and organized, leading to inefficient use of capacity and processing power, and to occasionally unreliable output.

It was only when these risks were expressed as above that the benefits of avoiding them could be estimated. A value was attributed to each risk which the business would face were it to do nothing. And having better understood the nature of the problem, the solution became clearer. Instead of buying ever larger storage and processing capacity (which was itself part of the problem, not the solution), the organization would invest in a project to make more efficient use of the existing warehouse. The Business Case proposed that better governance was the solution, not more kit. An investment in managed processes, overseen and authorized by a body of data warehouse owners, would cost much less to deliver, and would result in a longer-lasting solution.

What began as yet another IT upgrade project ended as one delivering cross-organizational behavioural change.

What this means

Risk management begins as a state of mind

Had the organization failed to consider the real risks it faced, it would have continued to encounter the need to pay for increased hardware capacity and never tackled the underlying issues. Eventually, those issues would have revealed themselves in ways far more threatening to the business:

- In the absence of any ownership, the data warehouse would never become the strategic tool for revenue growth that the business wished it to be.
- The proliferation of users' ad hoc enquiries would prevent critical jobs from running.
- Control of the IT budget would have been lost as unpredictable demands were made of it.
- Use of the database by the very people it was meant to serve would have been curtailed in order to limit its growing inefficiency.
- The weak integrity of the data warehouse would result in poor quality output leading to unreliable conclusions.

'Risk management' and 'project management' are synonymous

Every project is an exercise in risk management because each one seeks to do something which is unique – even if only subtly so. It is the exclusive and distinctive features of projects which make each one risky. So, although the term 'project management' is freely and commonly used, what those who work in project environments are actually doing is continuously managing risk. All of the tools and techniques which have been described throughout this book have one purpose in mind: to mitigate the risk of a management failure.

The consequences of ignoring the imperative

In the midst of chaos, an executive once described to me how he managed the project through the 'issues log'. Had he managed it through the risks log, he might have had fewer problems on his plate.

Issues are merely risks which have not been identified or mitigated, which is not to say that every problem can be anticipated. However, when no attempt is made to understand the possible consequences of untoward future events, it is likely that managers will face costly, time-consuming and potentially benefit-threatening issues, none of which will make a positive contribution to project success.

There are many people like the executive above who work best when they are fixing problems. All organizations need such people because no organization can anticipate every problem it will face. But when this behaviour becomes part of the culture, greater prominence is given to those that fix the issues than to those who seek to prevent them happening. In such cultures, not only do projects tend to be poorly managed, but they also tend to hold a lesser status. In many such institutions, projects are simply not the vehicle of choice for delivering changes and therefore there is little if any evident project or risk management. The consequences of a failure to change can threaten the whole business.

As I've delighted in saying many times before: a little risk management saves an awful lot of fan-cleaning.

The solutions

Always consider the 'do nothing' option

As the Case study illustrated, projects may often be justified best by considering the risk of doing nothing. In fact, in many regulated organizations this is more often than not the case. The consequence of failing to implement a legally mandated change could result in the business's inability to trade, so the case for such a project is easily made.

There are other categories of project which are best justified in the same way. Many organizations failed to obtain the business engagement they needed when concerns about the 'millennium bug' were first raised. Commercial people could see only the escalating IT costs of the proposed work and sought to reduce them. It was only when the problem was expressed as a risk to the entire business's viability that it was taken seriously. If a company was unable to operate on 1 January 2000, the shareholders would be holding the chief executive to account, not the IT director.

Yet even after that change of perspective had been taken, a continued risk-centric approach allowed the business to exercise some control over what might otherwise have been an even more expensive initiative. Many organizations treated all of their IT systems with equal priority; in their eyes, they all had to be fixed. Yet those with an eye on the risks prioritized those that mattered most, investing their immediate attention and resource on the business-critical computer systems which they could least afford to fail. So payroll and customer billing systems were considered before any other.

Other computer projects may be justified in a similar way. Business people have little interest in software upgrade projects, often characterizing them as initiatives which do not affect or interest them. So instead of attempting to cost-justify the often huge investments needed by offsetting them against productivity improvements from increased functionality, IT departments are most likely to gain the engagement of the business by putting a monetary figure against the costs of not upgrading. For instance, outdated systems often incur higher maintenance costs as experts become fewer and spare parts are less available. The longer an organization clings to ageing computers, the greater the risks – and costs – they will face.

New product and service developments are projects which traditionally attract an investment argument based on increased revenues yet which may be supported by an additional – and sometimes more powerful – risk-based argument. Once more, the 'do nothing' perspective is adopted, allowing the business to consider its prospects by failing to tackle its competitors, or forecasting the eventual downward trend of its own existing revenue stream. So if growth or revenue increases are considered sceptically, a better case may be made by describing the costs incurred in a world where competitors are stealing an increasing percentage of the business.

In any case, if you fail to sell a project to one audience by promoting its more upbeat, income-generating benefits, a risk-based
argument may resonate with a different community and result in
the investment you seek.

Build risk management into the project life cycle

Having introduced a risk-based mindset even before the project
has begun, it is crucial to drive it through the project. This means
not only ensuring that a process is in place to identify, prepare for
and mitigate risks, but that the importance of risk management
pervades the project environment and is recognized by everyone.
This requires the project's senior managers to adopt the mindset,
and actively promote it within the project's management environment. Simply delegating risk management to the Project Manager
may result in two undesirable consequences. First, it can be interpreted as no more than a need for a process which is to be followed
slavishly, without comprehension of the reason. Second, it places in
the hands of a single person the ownership of potential problems
which may be beyond their capability and authority to resolve. It is
quite acceptable to charge the Project Manager with the management of the process, but it often takes an entire organization to
identify and mitigate the risks which pass through that process.

The mechanics of a risk management process are relatively
straightforward. It is the principles and concepts that underpin the
process which are often easy for an organization to misunderstand.
The value and benefits of risk management lie in a deep comprehension of risk itself. This is why I continue to refer to the
importance of a risk mindset. For instance, I see many project plans
and many of them contain extensive lists of assumptions. From
one perspective, it is good to see that plans have been based on
articulated postulations. Yet these assumptions are only guesses
made by planners in place of facts. Here are some real examples:

- 'This project's priority will remain unchanged.'
- 'The requirements will remain stable throughout the project.'
- 'All resources required (human and non-human) will be made
  available.'

- 'We will secure all necessary funding.'
- 'Assigned resources will give precedence to this project rather than to BAU activity.'
- 'All resources will be competent to deliver what has been asked of them.'
- 'All dependencies with other projects, departments or suppliers will be honoured.'
- 'Current planned time slots will remain open.'

Each guess, each unknown, is a risk. So from another perspective, a list of assumptions suggests risk, whether for the project or in the construction of the plan or in the competence of the planner.

Sometimes, the earlier that planning has taken place, the longer the length of the list of project assumptions. This is not in itself a problem, merely a symptom of a usual human and commercial wish to know possible costs and timescales as soon as possible. But this also suggests that the earlier the forecast, the less reliable it will be. As the planning horizon extends ever further into an uncertain future, the increased risks of the unknown deserve to be offset with some mitigation. Therefore, some form of contingency should accompany any plan as compensation for the risk it contains.

As Figure 10.1 illustrates, as more becomes known about the project as it advances, the contingency needed can be progressively reduced to match the (hopefully!) reduced risk.

There are two ways in which a contingency budget may be calculated. One can accept a staged scale of mitigation which, although quite unspecific, serves as a common rule of thumb for all projects to apply. Simply put, at each project stage, a contingency representing a flat percentage of the estimated budget is added. For example, if project costs are being forecast during the Benefits Discovery phase, it might be considered sensible to add a contingency of 50 per cent. At initiation, given that more has become known about the project, the figure may be reduced to 30 per cent. During delivery, a 10 per cent contingency may be applied, and so on. This can work well in the very early stages of a project, but as more becomes known about its nature, adding round-figure

FIGURE 10.1

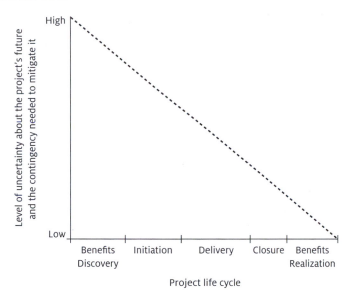

Project life cycle

percentages demonstrates a lack of understanding of the real risks which the project management team should properly understand. So the common alternative is to calculate it. A way of doing so is to estimate the cost of each risk's mitigation, and add to it the amount of change expected for a project of this nature, plus the cost of administering the change management process (as described in Chapter 6).

The usual form in which risks are captured is as illustrated in Figure 10.2. This is often called a Risk Register.

The risk is described by means of a clearly expressed cause-and-effect statement. For each risk, the likelihood (L) and impact (I) are estimated, and then multiplied to establish the factor (F). It is the risk factor which determines its relative criticality, and therefore who may be best assigned to approve and lead the mitigation efforts, as shown in Figure 10.3.

The mitigations available tend to fall into four categories and it can be helpful to think in these terms when considering how to tackle a potential problem. The categories are: Accept; Lessen;

FIGURE 10.2

RISK	L	I	F	MITIGATION	CONTINGENCY ($)
Delivery of equipment required for implementation will be delayed, resulting in delivery delay to client	8	7	56	Line up an alternative supplier	10,500
Key internal legal resource will be unavailable during summer leading to absence of essential input	2	7	14	Buy resource out of their holiday	2,500
Requirements change or are added after approval, resulting in impact on currently stated time and/or cost	8	5	40	Set aside change budget based on previous project Set aside change management budget based on previous project	35,500 10,000
TOTAL					58,500

FIGURE 10.3

Risk factor

Impact					
11	22	44	66	88	110
9	18	36	54	72	90
7	14	28	42	56	70
5	10	20	30	40	50
3	6	12	18	24	30
0	2	4	6	8	10

Likelihood

110	**assign to Change Management Team**
60–109	**assign to Project Steering Group**
20–59	**assign to Project Manager**
0–19	**assign to Work Stream Leader**

Avoid; Share. This forms the convenient (and possibly appropriate) acronym, ALAS.

Accept

Here, we simply accept that the risk may transpire but that we will do no more to mitigate it. In other words, by accepting the risk we have identified, we are treating it as though it were an *assumption*. Therefore, an assumption is a risk the project is prepared to take. This does not change the fact that the risk should be considered in terms of its likelihood and effect, but that the mitigation is to do nothing.

Lessen

It is possible to reduce the impact and/or likelihood of a risk. The specific mitigation may affect either the impact or the likelihood or both, so it is important to know what the outcome should be.

Avoid

Some risks can be circumvented. At the very least, the likelihood of a risk should be monitored carefully to determine whether it is moving towards being realized.

Share

Risks are often shared. For example, the likelihood and/or effect of a washing machine failing may be sufficiently high to justify taking out a service contract, so we share the risk with an insurer. Similarly, it is usual to share the risks and rewards of an initiative with a key supplier through penalty and reward clauses in contracts. For example, to mitigate the risk of the project going over budget, a customer might insist on compensation for every day by which the supplier exceeds a target completion date. However, sharing the risk does not always transfer the whole burden to someone else, as illustrated in the Case study.

How a project advances to the point at which it has such a register is usually as a culmination of risk management activity conducted through workshops to whom all supportive parties may be invited. It should fall to the sponsor to issue the invitations for such events and to ensure that they are used both to identify the risks and promote a risk-focused attitude. Thereafter, the Project Manager may pick up the process of continuing the important work. The materials to support such workshops are available on the Kogan Page website.

Develop a risk-focused culture

As with many of the practices described in this book, success depends upon their becoming customary. By driving and demonstrating such behaviours from the top, there is a greater likelihood that the principles and techniques will become embedded within the organization's culture. Following are some suggested behaviours one might expect from enlightened senior managers.

Encourage risk leadership

Make demands on Project Managers to engage with others to identify the risks and establish what mitigations may be possible. Ensure that the project sponsor sits at the head of the project's risk hierarchy, and that they accept their responsibility for directing what is, in effect, a risk-laden package of work. Don't expect the Project Manager to manage every potential problem; many mitigations may simply be beyond their limits of authority.

Invest in risk management

Encourage your Project Manager's careful calculation of contingency. Challenge it by all means, but do not simply discount it altogether. Allow them the time and opportunity during the project to identify the risks and to manage their mitigation.

Drive up the standards of risk management

Too often, the mechanics of risk management are followed with little or no attention to the quality of understanding. Challenge the quality of the description of risks. For instance, it is utterly unhelpful to see listed 'Resources get taken away' since this tells us nothing about which resources, why they may be removed or what would be the consequence. In fact, it is as unconstructive as the assumption listed earlier that 'all resources required will be made available'.

Make regular checks to ensure that the Risk Register is being used frequently and that the Project Manager and team can talk with understanding about the content. At meetings, do not only focus on the immediate issues, pressing as they may be. These may be causing you difficulty now for having been paid too little attention earlier.

When risk-moderating actions have been agreed upon, look for evidence that those actions are underway. The entire investment in risk management will have been wasted unless the mitigations are implemented.

Anticipate and mitigate post-project risks which may impact business as usual

Many risks which an institution may face might first be identified from within an individual project. Yet it is common for those involved in a project to look no further than the often limited horizon of its eventual date of completion. What happens beyond is wrongly considered someone else's problem.

During a project, it is possible to identify two types of risk: those which may impact the management and conduct of the project itself, and those which may affect the business after the project environment has been disbanded. The Risk Register listed a few examples of the former, but of the latter, there was no mention. This should not be the case as there are many things that a project may do to mitigate operational challenges which the business may face when the project has gone. For example, a project which sought to set up a supermarket's home delivery service anticipated operational challenges it would face such as vehicle breakdowns and road closures. Although these might have been considered problems with which the business would have to deal, the project contributed some mitigating solution by creating and handing over an operations handbook which described what might be done under such circumstances.

Conclusion

The Case study at the start of this chapter was chosen as a slightly unusual illustration of the way in which risk management can be used to great effect. A more conventional example might have described a project which, having been planned, identified the risks and delegated the mitigations across the team. Instead, an example was used to show how risk management is a way of looking at the world, and thus a discipline which may be brought to bear on business challenges even before a project exists.

SUMMARY

- Risk management is a crucial discipline, supported by a management process.
- Managing projects is an exercise in managing business risk.
- Considering the 'do nothing' option will help to reveal the business risks which a project must seek to overcome.
- Risk management is a continuous, pervading part of any organization's governance, and should be as embedded throughout the life cycle of every project as it is in the daily operation of the business.
- Contingency should not be considered a luxury, but as a fund which is planned to mitigate risks and pay for essential changes.
- The estimation of a risk's likelihood and impact allows for a 'factor' to be calculated which, in turn, helps to determine who should approve and lead the efforts to mitigate it.
- Risk management will not become an institutional habit unless its practice is driven by the most senior people in the organization.

CHAPTER ELEVEN

MAKING EFFECTIVE PROJECT MANAGEMENT SECOND NATURE

At the start of this book, I suggested that what we commonly think of as the causes of project failure are often the symptoms. The causes themselves often lie in behavioural failures of the institutions in which the projects are incubated and conducted. It follows that the solution for an entire organization lies in adapting its culture and behaviours to be more accommodating to the management of projects.

Those organizations which are effective in delivering successful business or sustainable change through projects are those where the governance to do so is so much a part of the culture that it becomes second nature to everyone.

However, the introduction of a new governance may itself represent a change for many people. Any approach to designing, implementing and embedding a new way of working must take account of the fact that it must be a culture-changing exercise if it is to succeed. If project management behaviours are not modified at a personal and organizational level, the desired transformation will simply not be realized.

The benefits to be derived from the introduction of a new form of management will take time to arrive. While waiting for them, the leaders of the change must be sure to carefully manage the expectations of those many stakeholders who will be affected by the outcome. For some, it may not be a palatable experience; their workload may increase, or they may be required to work in a way that is not instinctive. Others will relish the opportunity to embrace practices that enhance their professional lives. Those who seek to design, implement and embed the new approach will need to deliver an outcome which neither panders to, nor exiles, either of these two extremes. A managed approach is essential, so it is not surprising that the use of a project to introduce and embed project management into an organization can be a most effective delivery vehicle. Let's call it a Project Management Improvement Initiative (PMII).

Establishing the case for change

Many times in this book, I have referred to the link between projects and business change – one delivers the other. In promoting the case for the effective governance of projects, it must be clearly stated to all relevant stakeholders from the outset that an investment in project management will directly contribute to the organization's ability to meet its change agenda. Failure to communicate this message will simply result in their inability to see the relevance of the proposal. Here are some examples of business drivers to which effective project management may make a contribution:

- achieving demanding financial targets (both revenue generation and cost containment);
- overcoming competitive challenges;
- responding swiftly to change;
- being recognized for excellence in product and service delivery;
- providing opportunities for development to personnel.

The case for a PMII can be made more compelling by comparing the organization's existing project management capabilities to an index, thereby putting any aspirations into a context. This can also suggest how significant the journey may be to achieve the desired level of expertise. A Capability Maturity Model (CMM) provides some simple measures to determine an organization's state of development. Typically, there are five levels of maturity:

- Initial, where a chaotic, unstructured approach is self-evident. Success is dependent on a combination of chance and the personal energy of key drivers of change.
- Repeatable, where there is evidence of prior success being repeated.
- Defined, where a systemized approach to project management is evident and documented.
- Managed, where the approach is integrated with wider business management, and measurement of performance is possible.
- Optimized, where feedback from practice and innovation is incorporated into the organization's documented and cultural approach to project management such that it becomes self-improving and self-sustaining.

I have included on the Kogan Page website a CMM for project management, covering the topics contained in this book. Once judged, the analysis may be illustrated in a format like that shown in Figure 11.1. This example shows an organization's position on a simple scale of project management maturity. Despite some limited

FIGURE 11.1

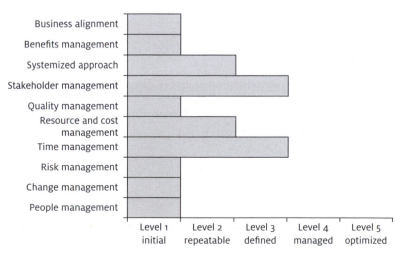

peaks, this organization's maturity is no more advanced than the lowest-measuring item, and is therefore level 1.

There are several maturity models for project management on the market. Amongst the more structured is the Project Management Institute's 'Organizational Project Management Maturity Model' (commonly referred to as 'OPM3'). It seeks to provide a way for organizations to understand organizational project management and to measure their maturity against a comprehensive and broad-based set of best practices. It also helps organizations that wish to increase their project management maturity to plan for improvement.

Although many potential sponsors may be persuaded by the impact of a comparison with an industry norm, many will wish to judge their organization's improvements against their own past performance. In this way, they will see advancement in project management being measured in more relevant, and possibly commercial, terms.

A questionnaire can serve as a helpful tool to identify and consolidate the perceptions of a varied audience. One has been included on the Kogan Page website, listing a range of statements to which survey participants may anonymously respond on a scale of 1 to 9, allowing them to show the extent to which they disagree or agree with each. The consolidation of the results of such a survey paints a picture of the concerns of different levels of management at a point in time, thereby providing an indication of where the organization's priorities lie, and a further mandate for change. Further surveys can be conducted during the life of the PMII to determine the extent to which improvements are being realized.

Dependent upon the audiences that have been invited to participate, the outcome of the analysis may identify some clear but probably contradictory priorities. For instance, potential sponsors may strongly agree with the statement: 'Projects routinely miss time, cost and quality targets.' Project Managers may strongly agree with the statement: 'Expectations fluctuate so much that we are rarely able to state the scope of our projects with any certainty.' The solution lies in a carefully planned and unified approach to the delivery of improvements.

Obtaining a mandate for change

It is not sufficient that the opportunities for change can be clearly expressed. A sponsor, or sponsors, will be needed to drive, fund and direct the PMII. The more senior they are in the organization, the better. However, this is not to say that anyone will be suitable. Nor is it enough that there is a groundswell of enthusiasm for change. Without sponsorship, the initiative will either fail to start successfully, or will falter soon after. If the PMII is to be managed according to the principles of effective project management, those principles may be applied to the selection of a suitable Project Steering Group to own and direct it.

The sponsor must be a recognized promoter of change, ideally someone who has previously sponsored significant change initiatives for the organization. They should be senior enough to command the respect and engagement of their peers since their role will involve selling and promoting concepts that may be alien or unpalatable to others. Significantly, they should have access to funds and be prepared to commit them over what may be a lengthy period of time. Ideally, the sponsor will have been the one to initially identify the need for change and to have driven the PMII this far.

The Specialist authority must be a recognized expert in the management of projects. This is not merely to say that they should be a competent manager of change; their abilities must extend to understanding intimately the 'systemized approach' since they must assure the organization that it will be a robust and reliable solution to its challenges. It is sometimes the case that this specialist will be sourced from outside the organization since this is where the expertise may lie. A project management consultant may suit such a role. It is possible that a second individual may be necessary where the organization already has a significant number or complexity of existing systems and processes into which the project management approach is to be accommodated. This second candidate may come from the finance department since this is from where so many management processes derive.

The User authority must ensure that the delivered solution meets the needs of the organization. It is sensible to accommodate two individuals who represent communities that will be affected differently by the PMII's outcome, namely the organization's sponsors and its project managers. Therefore, a well-respected Project Manager and sponsor can be included as User authorities in the PMII's Project Steering Group to ensure that, whatever the solution, it satisfies these two parties.

To ensure that the PMII is well planned, monitored and controlled, much will depend upon the selection of an appropriate Project Manager. They can also act as a beacon for best practice – if the PMII is itself poorly managed, there will be little chance of the benefits it seeks to promote becoming entrenched elsewhere. If the organization does not yet have a candidate with the necessary qualifications, the individual may be selected from elsewhere, typically a project management consultancy. The commitment to a suitable individual should not be underestimated; dependent upon the scale of change desired, a PMII for a medium-sized organization may take upwards of two years to complete.

With a powerful, guiding coalition in place (if only informally at this stage), and an identified Project Manager waiting to be instructed, the fledgling PMII is ready to use the evidence it has gathered to justify its case for change.

Justifying the investment

A comparison of current and future states might make an emotive case for change, but most organizations should look for commercial benefits to be delivered by a PMII. Too often, the change is instigated by junior levels of management who argue that a consistent approach to project management will inherently deliver rewards. However, this is not an argument that adequately supports the investment of what may be a large sum of money. That everyone is working in a common way will, at best, allow the avoidance of rework, but will not be the reasoning that persuades the senior management team to adopt the initiative. Instead, having sold the concept to the wider senior management team, those promoting the PMII should build a substantial Business Case which shows the range of varied benefits that may be realized from the adoption of effective project management governance.

Like most projects, the benefits of a PMII typically fall into three categories – revenue generation, cost containment or productivity improvement, and risk mitigation. All of these, when considered together, make a more persuasive case in favour of investment. An example of the benefits that may be anticipated, and the means by which they could be quantified, are available on the Kogan Page website. It is by no means an exhaustive list and although it suggests how the benefits of a PMII may be articulated, it is highly probable that the figures quoted will be disputed. This is most likely to be due to the fact that they are, like any plan, a forecast and therefore open to debate. After discussion, the proposed revenue increases, cost savings and mitigation of risks may well have been diminished. However, they should ideally outweigh the proposed costs of the PMII, which may be substantial. In any case, if the culture of the organization is closed to the use of a disciplined project management approach, it is unlikely that any Business Case will persuade them otherwise. In such a case, unpalatable as it may seem, it may be necessary to wait until events arise (such as a failure to deliver a project) which force the issue.

Delivering the change

In Figure 1.2 in Chapter 1, I identified some essential components that allow for the effective management of projects. The model I used is refined in Figure 11.2 to account for what has been covered in the intervening chapters, and to suggest an order in which they may be implemented.

Although every organization is different, the order in which these components become understood and entrenched often begins with a mechanism for business priority management – what was described in Chapter 2 as a Change Management Team, and its supporting governance. Thereafter, a clockwise progression tends to be

FIGURE 11.2

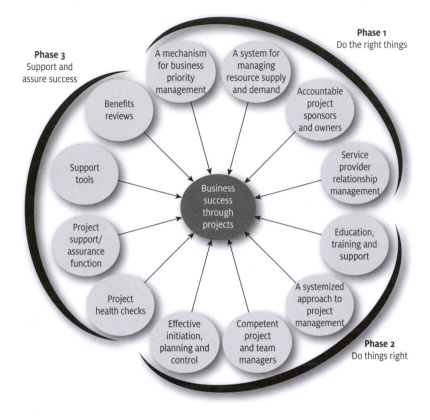

both logical and benefit-driven, concluding with the most mature organizations conducting Benefit Reviews. With this outline sequence in mind, a plan can emerge. The Project Manager must consider that in order for the desired future state to be reached, these components must be selected, sequenced and delivered. It is suggested that these components may be addressed in the three phases identified, forming a progressively firmer foundation for future enhancements of the approach to project management.

Phase 1 is characterized by the importance of selecting, commissioning and funding the right projects. This includes generating an enthusiasm and competence amongst senior managers such that they may commission and lead projects that will deliver their strategic imperatives. This will require the commitment of service providers from both within and outside the organization.

This phase must also succeed in delivering some successful projects! Without some early wins to promote the approach, few will see the benefit of the investment. It follows that in selecting projects to which the approach is to be applied, the timing of such projects is carefully considered. This will ensure that there are milestones throughout the PMII which demonstrate the value it is delivering.

Only after having ensured that the right projects have been chosen and assigned to accountable executives should an investment be made in Phase 2. This phase is characterized by a need to initiate, plan, monitor and control projects according to a robust, reliable and systematic approach. In this way, the management of individual projects within the portfolio becomes the focus.

The organization-wide training and education programme which is often commissioned at huge expense at the beginning of a PMII now becomes important as a tool through which not only to educate, but to promote and sell the benefits to everyone. Priority should be given to sponsors and other senior stakeholders who must persuade others to adopt the approach. To train Project Managers too early is to waste both a precious opportunity and resource. Trainees will return from their courses, enthusiastic and capable, yet thrust into an environment that has not yet caught up with them. It is for this reason that the placement of training and education must be carefully considered, using the following criteria:

- Can potential trainees be prioritized according to their seniority? A first round of 'senior management briefings' will be essential if the drive for change is to come from the top of the organization. The use of the term 'briefing' as opposed to 'training' is important since it takes account of the sensitivities of executives who may believe that, for them, training is unnecessary. Trainees should be selected from a carefully considered, prioritized range of participants.

- Can potential trainees be prioritized according to the importance of the projects in which they are engaged? Some projects may benefit if their participants are trained in project management. However, others may be at such a critical point that the introduction of a new approach to project management may do more damage than good. Trainees should be selected from a carefully considered, prioritized range of projects.

- Can potential trainees be prioritized according to their development needs? There will be those for whom an introduction to project management will represent an invaluable boost to their confidence and competence. There will be others for whom this will not be the case; in fact, the training may frustrate them or exacerbate existing issues. That people of all backgrounds and expertise will be involved in projects does not mean that they must all be trained in the principles and techniques of project management. It is better to focus on those for whom the management of projects is an essential competence. In the early stages at least, this may rule out the need to train and educate those who are not involved in the project's management. Trainees should be selected after careful consideration of their development needs.

So a common range of training for an organization will often include the following:

- Sponsor's Project Management Briefing. To familiarize project sponsors with their obligations such that they may clearly communicate amongst one another, and consistently direct the organization's community of project managers.
- Practitioner's Project Management. To provide practitioners with the skills and knowledge to practise the principles and techniques of project management in the organization.
- Condensed Project Management Overview. To provide non-participant personnel with sufficient knowledge that they may understand the principles of project management and the organization's approach to its application.
- Operational Project Management Techniques. To provide non-participant personnel with sufficient skills to practise the techniques of project management in operational areas of the organization.

These four events allow all potential delegates from project and operational backgrounds to obtain sufficient knowledge and/or skills to participate constructively in a project-focused environment.

Phase 3 sees the inclusion of some greater infrastructure to support and assure the organization. A sensible tactic is to support both the projects and the people who are being subjected to the new approach. This helps to ensure that the organization develops healthy projects and healthy project participants. Therefore, healthy projects are encouraged by the use of health checks and other assurance measures, whilst healthy project participants are encouraged to develop and flourish through support and guidance from the wider project management community. Since the introduction of project support and some supporting technology will inevitably require significant outlay and disruption, it is important that the investment so far has delivered some measurable rewards.

With the enactment of project Benefits Reviews, Phase 3 may not only represent a conclusion to the PMII, but also suggests that a significant level of organizational maturity has been reached. Desirable as it may be to conduct Benefits Reviews in Phase 1, it is unlikely that the essential principles that underpin the approach to project management will be sufficiently and widely enough understood to allow that to happen. It is only because an investment to develop, build and embed an approach to project management has been made in the two previous phases that it is culturally acceptable, and possible, to measure realized benefits.

Enjoying the benefits

The introduction of any new approach or method into an organization is, above all else, a change to its management culture. In his book *Leading Change*, John Kotter memorably remarked: 'In the final analysis, change sticks when it becomes "the way we do things around here", when it seeps into the bloodstream of the corporate body. Until new behaviours are rooted in social norms and shared values, they are subject to degradation as soon as the pressure for change is removed.'

The pressure to optimize competence in project management must not only be continuous and unrelenting but entire across all parties, including those service providers who may well be outside your immediate span of control. It takes entire organizations to deliver a project; no single individual or group can do it by themselves. It follows that those who seek to promote and embed the benefits of well governed projects must commit to what may be a lengthy and challenging process. It is only in this way that the underlying beliefs and values which dictate the behaviour of those involved in projects may be changed. Projects will never be easy to govern, but in nearly every case, they can be governed more easily. Just try applying some of what I very much hope you have learned from this book, and enjoy the benefits for yourself!

INDEX

NB: page numbers in *italic* indicate figures

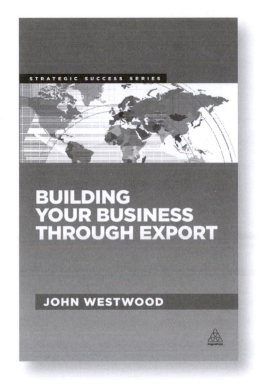

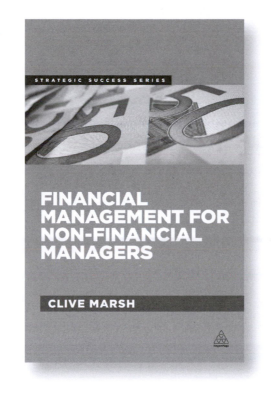